At the back of this book:
Updated Indiana Academic Standards for Reading, Writing, Listening, and Speaking!

Reading STREET

Indiana

Program Authors

Peter Afflerbach	Jeanne Paratore
Camille Blachowicz	P. David Pearson
Candy Dawson Boyd	Sam Sebesta
Wendy Cheyney	Deborah Simmons
Connie Juel	Sharon Vaughn
Edward Kame'enui	Susan Watts-Taffe
Donald Leu	Karen Kring Wixson

Editorial Offices: Glenview, Illinois • Parsippany, New Jersey • New York, New York
Sales Offices: Boston, Massachusetts • Duluth, Georgia • Glenview, Illinois
Coppell, Texas • Sacramento, California • Mesa, Arizona

We dedicate Reading Street to
Peter Jovanovich.

His wisdom, courage,
and passion for education
are an inspiration to us all.

About the Cover Artist
Daniel Moreton lives in New York City, where he uses his computer to create illustrations for books. When he is not working, Daniel enjoys cooking, watching movies, and traveling. On a trip to Mexico, Daniel was inspired by all of the bright colors around him. He likes to use those colors in his art.

ISBN: 0-328-26107-6

Copyright © 2008 Pearson Education, Inc.

1 2 3 4 5 6 7 8 9 10 V063 15 14 13 12 11 10 09 08 07 06

Dear Indiana Reader,

Scott Foresman Reading Street has many corners and crossroads. At each corner you will learn about something new and interesting. You will read about great ideas in science and social studies. You will have fun reading about clever chicks and smart mice detectives!

You may want to hurry down the street and read these wonderful stories and articles! But slow down, take your time, and enjoy yourself! You never know whom you might meet on *Reading Street!*

Sincerely,
The Authors

Great Ideas

Read It ONLINE sfsuccessnet.com

What difference can a great idea make?

Clever Solutions

Tippy-Toe Chick, GO!

Ideas That Changed the World

Great Ideas

What difference can a great idea make?

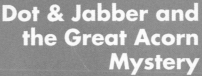

9

Let's Talk About
Clever Solutions

Words to Read

along
behind
toward
eyes
never
pulling

Read the Words

The chicks walked along the path behind the house. They walked toward the garden. Their eyes popped open! They saw a big dog that they had never seen before. It was barking and pulling on its leash.

Tippy-Toe Chick, GO!

Genre: Animal Fantasy
The animal characters in an animal fantasy act like people. In the next story you will read about a smart little chick who surprises her family.

Tippy-Toe

by George Shannon
illustrated by Laura Dronzek

Chick, GO!

What great idea
will Little Chick have?

Every morning when the dew had dried, Hen took her chicks to the garden for their favorite treat—sweet itty-bitty beans and potato bugs.

Hen, Big Chick, and Middle Chick next, with Little Chick trailing along behind. Stopping to wonder at this and that.

Then running, *tippy-toe, tippy-toe,* to catch the rest. Across the yard. Into the garden to eat, eat, eat. Every day, every day of the week.

Till ONE day—

RUFF-RUFF-RUFF-RUFF-RUFF!

A big, grumpy dog came running their way, barking and growling at the end of a rope.

Hen jumped back and pulled her chicks near. "There's no safe way to the beans today. We'll just have to wait for chicken feed."

All three chicks said, "Bleck!" and frowned.

"We're hungry!"

"You PROMISED!"

"We DID our chores!"

Hen sighed. "But
we'll NEVER get past
a dog like that."

19

Big Chick said, "Wait. I'LL take care of this."
He slowly took a step toward Dog. "Now listen,"
he called. "We won't hurt you. We're just going
to the garden for an itty-bitty treat."

RUFF-RUFF-RUFF-RUFF-RUFF!

Dog disagreed, barking and pulling at the end of his rope. Big Chick ran to hide under Hen's safe wing.

Middle Chick took a breath, then stepped toward Dog. "I'M hungry, so YOU'D better stop it right now! Or YOU'LL be sorry when we get hold of you."

RUFF-RUFF-RUFF-RUFF-RUFF!

Dog disagreed, barking and pulling at the end
of his rope. Middle Chick ran to hide under
Hen's safe wing.

"Let's go," said Hen. "We'll really have to wait."

Little Chick peeped, "*I* want to try."

"Oh, no!" said Hen, as the other chicks laughed. "You're much too small."

Little Chick yelled, "But *I* can RUN!" And off she went, *tippy-toe, tippy-toe,* as fast as she could. Straight toward Dog.

Hen screamed and grabbed her heart.

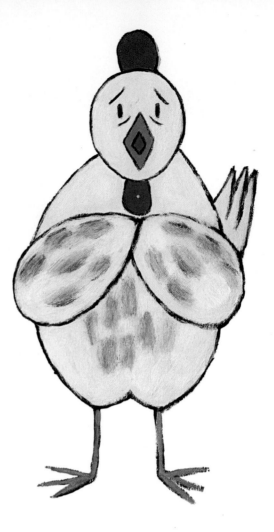

Big Chick closed his eyes.

Middle Chick shook.

Little Chick ran, *tippy-toe, tippy-toe,* without stopping to rest till she felt Dog's breath.

Then Little Chick laughed and began to run again. *Tippy-toe, tippy-toe* around the tree.

Dog chased after her, tugging at his rope. **RUFF-RUFF-RUFF-RUFF-RUFF!**

Tippy-toe, tippy-toe around the tree. *Tippy-toe, tippy-toe, tippy* . . . **RUFF-RUFF-RUFF!**

Around and around, *tippy-toe, tippy-toe.* Till . . .

RUFF-RUP-yip-yip-yip-yip!

Dog's rope was wrapped all around the tree.
He was stuck and too mad to think "back up."

Hen clucked with pride. Big Chick and Middle
Chick just stood and stared.

Little Chick called, "It's time to eat!"

And off they ran, *tippy-toe, tippy-toe.* Right past Dog and into the garden for their favorite treat—sweet itty-bitty beans and potato bugs.

"YUM!"

Think and Share

Talk About It What would you say to Little Chick about her great idea?

1. The pictures below are mixed up. Decide in which order they belong. Then use them to retell the story.

2. Where does Little Chick live? What words would you use to describe her?

3. What happened to Little Chick and her family at the beginning of the story? What happened at the end?

Look Back and Write Why was Little Chick's idea great? Look at pages 28–31.

Meet the Author
George Shannon

George Shannon is a tall man, but he likes little things. One of his favorite sayings is "Less is more." Does that sound like a good lesson for Little Chick?

Mr. Shannon likes to tell stories. He says, "I want my stories to sound as if they are being told out loud."

Read more books by George Shannon.

Belling the Cat

a fable adapted from Aesop
illustrated by Viviana Garofoli

The mice had a problem. There was a new cat in the house. It slept by the kitchen table. It hid behind doors. It raced down the hall toward the mice.

They could see its eyes in the dark.
They could hear it howl at night. They never
felt safe!

The mice called a meeting. They had many ideas.

One little mouse pulled on his ear and said, "We need to hear that cat. Let's hang a bell on its neck."

All the mice went along with the idea.
They cheered and clapped. They danced
and laughed.

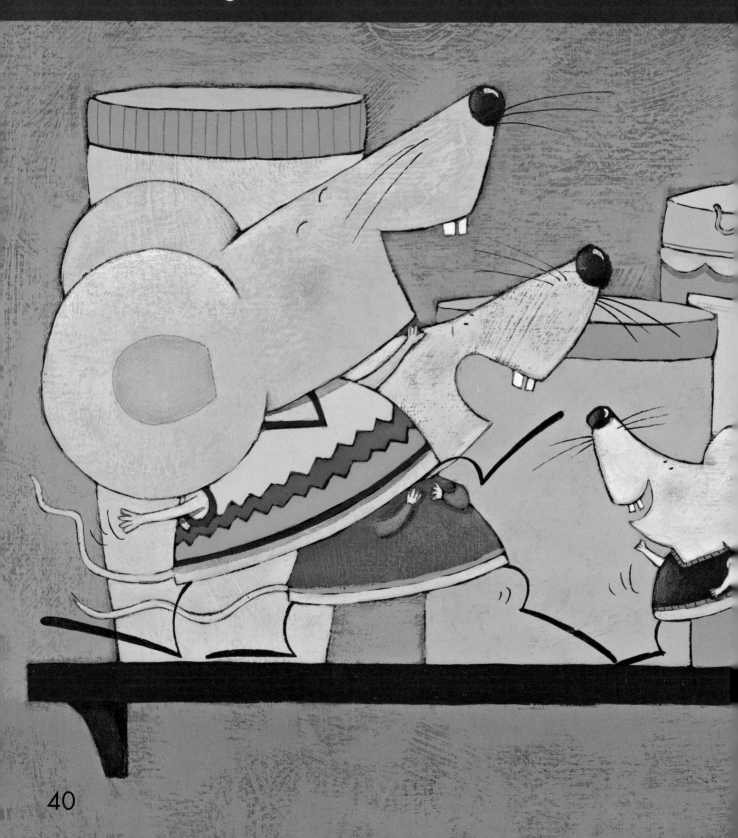

Then a wise old mouse asked, "Who is going to bell the cat?"

Moral: Some things are easier said than done.

Commands

A **command** is a sentence that tells someone to do something. It begins with a capital letter. It ends with a **period (.)**.

Come back, Little Chick**.**

Please go away, Dog**.**

42

Write Using Commands

1. Read these sentences. Write the sentence that is a command.

The big dog growled.
Run fast.

. . . .

2. Write these sentences again. Make them commands. Use capital letters and periods.

Will you please do your chores now?
Will you walk the dog?

. . . .

3. Imagine you are training your dog. Write commands telling your dog what to do. Use capital letters and periods.

Let's Talk About

Clever
Solutions

Words to Read

loved
wood
should
door

Read the Words

Mole loved the baby bird he found. He put it in a cage made of wood. What should Mole do? Should he keep the baby bird, or should he open the cage door and let the bird go?

Mole and the Baby Bird

Genre: Animal Fantasy
In an animal fantasy, the animal characters talk and act like people. The next story is about a mole who finds and takes care of a wild bird.

Mole and the Baby Bird

by Marjorie Newman
illustrated by Patrick Benson

What can Mole learn from a baby bird?

Mole found a baby bird.
It had fallen out of its nest.

Mole waited and waited: but no
big bird came to help it—so Mole
took the baby bird home.

He made a nest for it.
"Look!" he said to his mother.

"It's very, very hard to take care of a baby
bird," she said.

"They usually die," said his dad.

"My bird won't die," said Mole.

His friends helped him find food
for the baby.

His mother showed him how to feed it.
Mole fed it whenever it chirped.

And the bird didn't die! It grew.
"It's my pet bird," said Mole.
"It's not a pet bird. It's a wild bird,"
said his mother.

The bird fluttered its wings.

"Your bird is trying to fly," said his mother.

"No!" cried Mole. "It mustn't fly!"

Mole found some wood and some nails.
He borrowed his dad's toolbox.

"What are you making?" asked his dad.
"I'm making a cage for my pet bird!"
said Mole.

"It's not a pet bird. It's a wild bird,"
said his dad. "You should let it fly."
"No!" cried Mole.

He put his bird into its new cage.
The bird was sad.

Mole's mother was sad too. But Mole
kept his bird, because he loved it.

Then–Grandad came to visit. He looked at Mole's pet bird.

Presently Grandad said, "Let's go for a walk, little Mole."

Grandad took Mole to the top of a high hill.

Mole looked down at the trees far below.

He felt the wild wind trying to lift him.
"Wheee! I'm flying!" cried Mole.
"Nearly," said Grandad.

When Mole got home he looked at his bird. It was sitting very still in its cage in Mole's dark underground room. "Birds are meant to fly," said Mole.

He opened the cage door, and he let his bird
fly away because he loved it. Then he cried.

The next day Mole went into the forest.
He saw his bird flying, soaring, free. And Mole
was glad.

Read Together

Think and Share

Talk About It What lesson did Mole learn? Was it a good lesson to learn? Why do you think so?

1. Use the pictures below to retell the story of *Mole and the Baby Bird.*

2. Tell two things that happened after Mole found the baby bird.

3. How did Mole change at the end of the story?

Look Back and Write Mole tries to treat the baby bird like a pet. Look back at the story. What did he do? Make a list.

Meet the Author and the Illustrator

Marjorie Newman

Marjorie Newman lives in England. As a child, she often brought home caterpillars and tadpoles. When they turned into butterflies and frogs, she let them go.

Patrick Benson

Patrick Benson tries to show different views in his art. Can you find a picture that shows how the world looks to a flying bird?

Read another book by Marjorie Newman or illustrated by Patrick Benson.

Dear Dr. Know-It-All

by Paulinda Lynk

Dear Dr. Know-It-All,
My sister never knocks on my door. She just barges into my room. What should I do?
Getting Mad

Dear Getting Mad:

Tape a knock-knock joke to the wood on your door. Your sister will stop and read it! After that, I bet she will knock.

Dr. Know-It-All

69

Dear Dr. Know-It-All,
I loved your idea!
And it worked.
I even found a book
of knock-knock jokes
to keep her knocking!
Not Mad Now

Knock-
Knock

Knock! Knock!
Who's There?
Boo.
Boo who?
Why are you crying?

More Knock-Knock Jokes

Knock-knock.
Who's there?
Orange.
Orange who?
Orange you glad to see me?

Knock-knock.
Who's there?
Olive.
Olive who?
Olive to play with you!

Knock-knock.
Who's there?
Who.
Who who?
When did you get an owl?

Knock-knock.
Who's there?
Les.
Les who?
Les be friends!

Read Together

Exclamations

An **exclamation** is a sentence that shows strong feeling. It begins with a **capital letter.** It ends with an exclamation mark **(!).**

Mole has strong feelings about the baby bird. He wants to keep it. How would Mole say this sentence?

"**I**t mustn't fly**!**" cried Mole.

Write Using Exclamations

1. Write these exclamations. Use capital letters and exclamation marks correctly.

   we love our pet bird
   our bird just fell out of its nest

· ·

2. Look in *Mole and the Baby Bird.* Find another sentence that is an exclamation. Write it.

· ·

3. Choose a kind of bird. Write about it. Use some exclamations.

Let's Talk About
Clever
Solutions

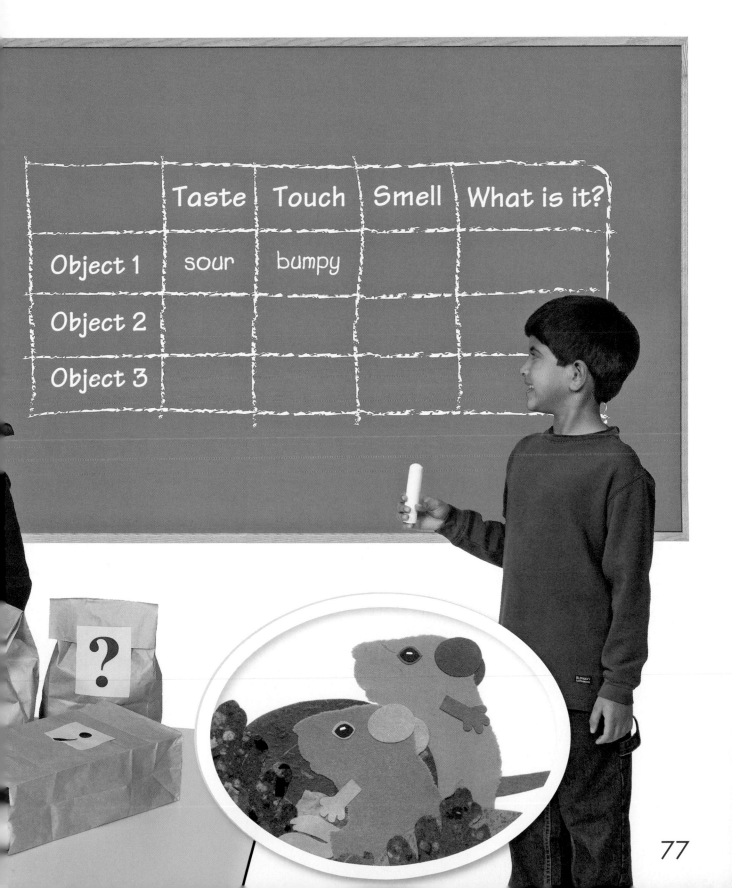

	Taste	Touch	Smell	What is it?
Object 1	sour	bumpy		
Object 2				
Object 3				

Words to Read

among
instead
another
none

Read the Words

We looked outside. A squirrel found an acorn among the leaves. He didn't eat it. Instead, he dug a hole and put the acorn in it. Then the squirrel found another acorn. None of us saw where he put that one.

Dot & Jabber
and the Great Acorn Mystery

Genre: Informational Fiction
Informational fiction tells a make-believe story, but it also gives facts and information that are true. The next story is a mystery about trees and how they grow where they do.

Dot & Jabber

and the Great Acorn Mystery

by Ellen Stoll Walsh

How will Dot and Jabber solve this mystery?

The detectives had nothing to do.

"We need a mystery to solve," said Jabber.

"Here's a mystery," said Dot. "What is this little oak tree doing here?"

"Why is that a mystery?" Jabber wanted
to know.

"Because of the acorn," said Dot. "How did
it get here?"

"Dot," said Jabber, "what acorn?"

"Acorns are oak tree seeds. This little oak tree grew from an acorn, and acorns come from big oak trees."

"Oh, *that* acorn," said Jabber. "But where's the big oak tree?"

"That's part of the mystery," said Dot. "Let's look for clues."

"Okay!" shouted Jabber. "Because we're detectives!" He poked his head into a hole.

"Hey, this is *my* hole," said a mole. "Go away. There are no clues down here. Try the big oak tree—on the *other* side of the meadow."

"Of course!" said Dot. "Come on, Jabber!"

"That's a long, long way," said Jabber.
"How did our acorn get from there to here?
Do you think it walked?"

"Let's find out," said Dot. "The acorn began at the big oak tree. So will we."

The detectives set off across the meadow.

After a while Jabber said, "I'm tired. Can we wonder about all these maple seeds instead?"

"There's no mystery in maple seeds," said Dot. "They have wings that twirl, and they ride the wind across the meadow."

"Maybe our acorn rode the wind too,"
said Jabber.

"That is what we are going to find out,"
said Dot.

At last they arrived at the big oak tree. "Look!" said Dot. "I bet there are a million acorns here."

"They don't have wings," said Jabber.
"But they taste good."
  "Don't eat them, Jabber! They're clues."

"Acorns don't have wings, but they might have sneaky feet," said Dot. "Let's keep watch and see if they start to move."

Plip. An acorn dropped from the big oak tree.

Jabber poked it with a stick. "This acorn isn't going anywhere," he said. "None of them are."

A squirrel came and sat down among
the acorns.

"Jabber, look!" Dot whispered. "What is
he doing?"

"Oh!" gasped Jabber. "He's eating our clue!"

"He can't be," said Dot. "The shell is still
on it."

"So why is he stuffing it in his mouth?" asked Jabber.

The squirrel ran off.

"Oh no, he's stealing the acorn!" the detectives cried and ran after him.

When the squirrel stopped, they stopped and watched to see what would happen next.

"What's he doing now?" asked Jabber.

"Digging a hole. Look! He's hiding the acorn."

Jabber stared at Dot. "Maybe he's planting it!"

"Of course!" said Dot. "Our acorn crossed the meadow on squirrel feet."

"And got planted by squirrel feet," said Jabber.

"And grew into the little oak tree," said Dot. "The mystery is solved. We are two clever mouse detectives!"

"Hurray!" shouted Jabber. "Now what will we do?"

"Find another mystery," said Dot.

"But I'm hungry," said Jabber. "First let's go eat some of those leftover clues."

Think and Share

Talk About It Dot and Jabber are detectives. Why are they good at what they do?

1. Use the pictures below to summarize what you learned about seeds.

2. Oak tree seeds, or acorns, are different from maple tree seeds. Tell how.

3. Did you have trouble as you read? What did you do? How did that help?

Test Practice

Look Back and Write What was the answer to the great acorn mystery? Look back at page 99.

Meet the Author and Illustrator

Ellen Stoll Walsh

Ellen Stoll Walsh grew up in a big family. She was one of ten children! It was fun but noisy. She liked to read books to get away from the noise.

Now Ms. Walsh writes books. She cuts paper to make the art. In her books, she tells stories and teaches facts about the world.

Read more books by Ellen Stoll Walsh.

Dot & Jabber
and the Mystery of the Missing Stream

Ellen Stoll Walsh

Mouse Magic
Ellen Stoll Walsh

More color magic by the creator of Mouse Paint!

Water

Our class did an experiment. We observed changes in water. Here's what we did.

1. We put water in a cup.
2. We marked it with a line.
3. We waited one week.
4. We took notes.

We looked at the cup. We drew another line to mark the water. The water went down. Where did it go? None of us knew.

Our teacher said that the water went into the air. It is there, but we can't see it. This is called evaporation.

We decided to do another experiment. This time we put the water among the plants instead of in the sun. What will happen? We will check for evaporation in a week.

How Sentences Begin and End

A **sentence** is a group of words that tells a complete idea. It begins with a **capital letter**. A statement ends with a **period (.)**. A **question** ends with a **question mark (?)**.

Acorns are oak tree seeds**.**

This sentence is a statement. It tells something.

How did this oak tree get here**?**

This sentence is a question. It asks something.

Write Using Sentences

1. Write these sentences. Use capital letters and end marks correctly.

   oak trees grow from acorns
   how do maple trees grow

· ·

2. Find a statement and a question in *Dot & Jabber and the Great Acorn Mystery.* Write the sentences.

· ·

3. What do you want to know about trees? Write a question. Then answer the question. Use capital letters and end marks correctly.

Let's Talk About

Ideas That Changed the World

Words to Read

goes
kinds
heavy
against
today

Read the Words

The forklift goes back and forth. It lifts all kinds of heavy boxes. It stacks them against the wall. The boxes will be shipped today.

Genre: Expository Nonfiction
Expository nonfiction explains something. The next selection explains how simple machines make work easier.

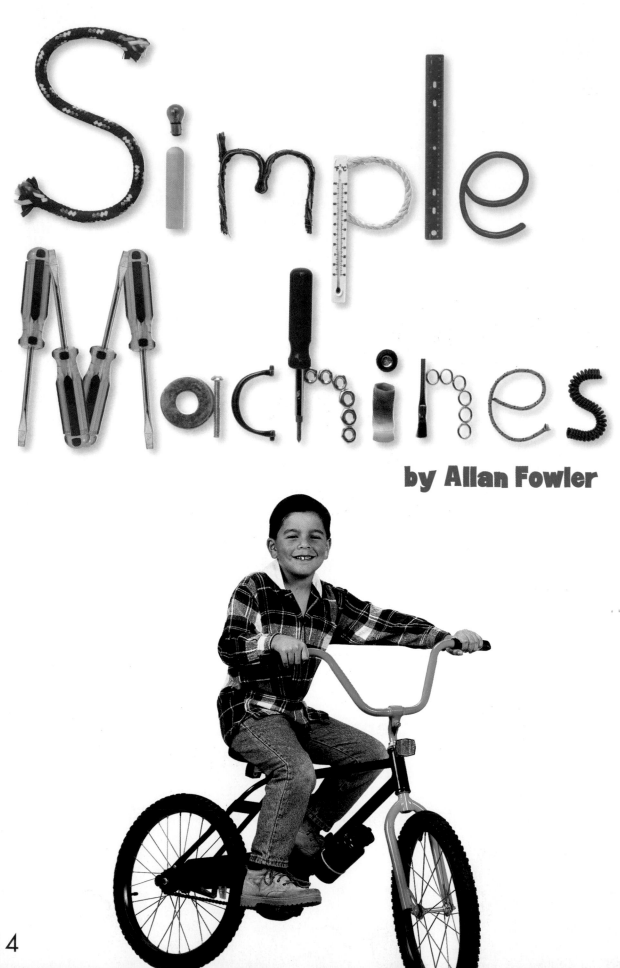

Simple Machines

by Allan Fowler

How do simple machines help us?

We use machines every day. Machines help make our lives easier.

Some machines, such as lawn mowers and vacuum cleaners, have many parts.

vacuum cleaner

lawn mower

Other machines have few parts. They are called simple machines. Levers, inclined planes, wheels and axles, and pulleys are four kinds of simple machines.

These everyday things are simple machines.

This bottle opener is a kind of lever.
It helps you remove the cap from a bottle.

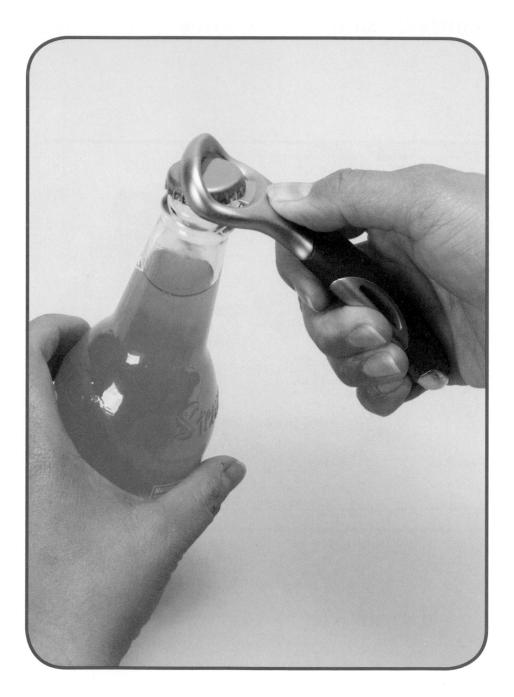

Some levers can help you move a heavy object, such as a rock.

This boy is using a lever called a crowbar.

Push down on one end of a lever. The other end moves up and pushes against whatever you are trying to move.

Have you ever ridden a seesaw?

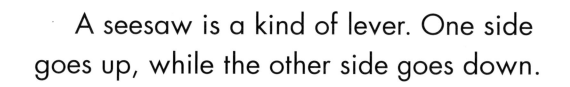

A seesaw is a kind of lever. One side goes up, while the other side goes down.

Inclined planes are all around you.

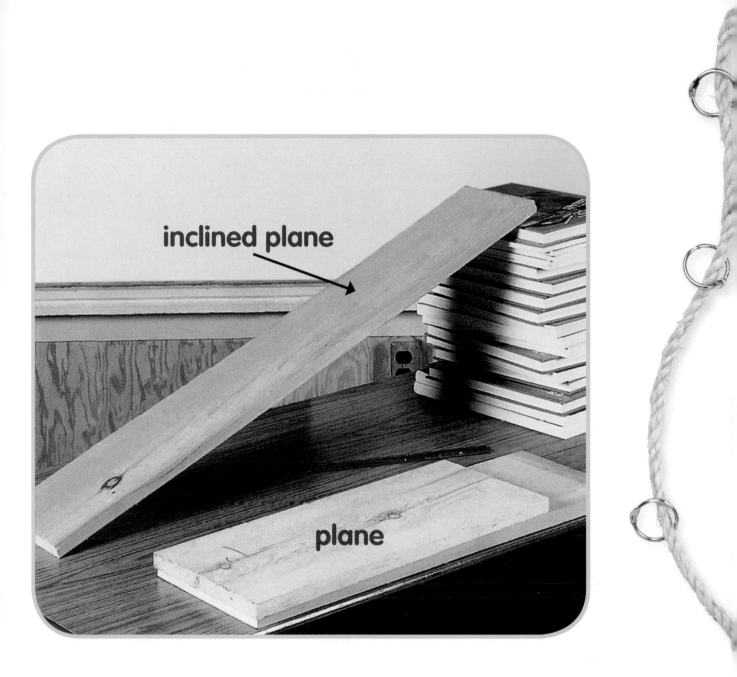

A plane is just a flat surface, like
a wooden board. An inclined plane
is a flat surface that is slanted.

Ramps are inclined planes. It is easier to push a big load up a ramp than to lift it.

A wedge is another kind of inclined plane.

wedge

A wedge can help you cut wood.
When a wedge is hit with a big
hammer, its thin part splits the wood.

Wheels help things go.

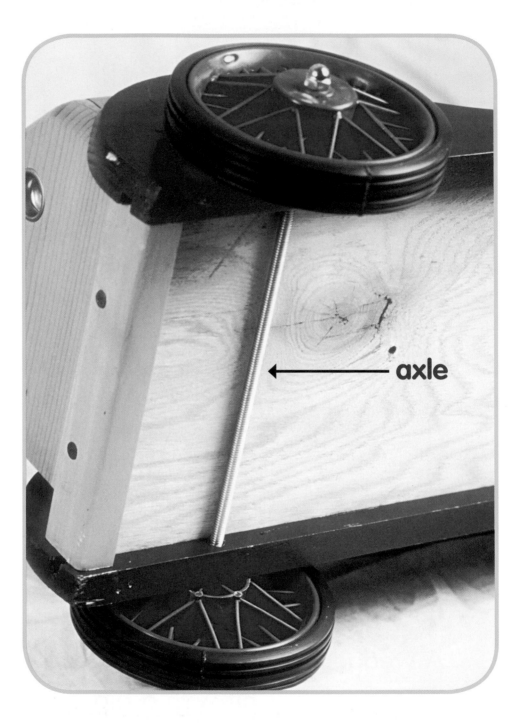

axle

An axle, or rod, connects a pair of wheels. The axle helps the wheels turn.

Wheels are on bicycles and cars.
It would be very hard to move a bike
or car without wheels.

127

A pulley helps you lift heavy objects.

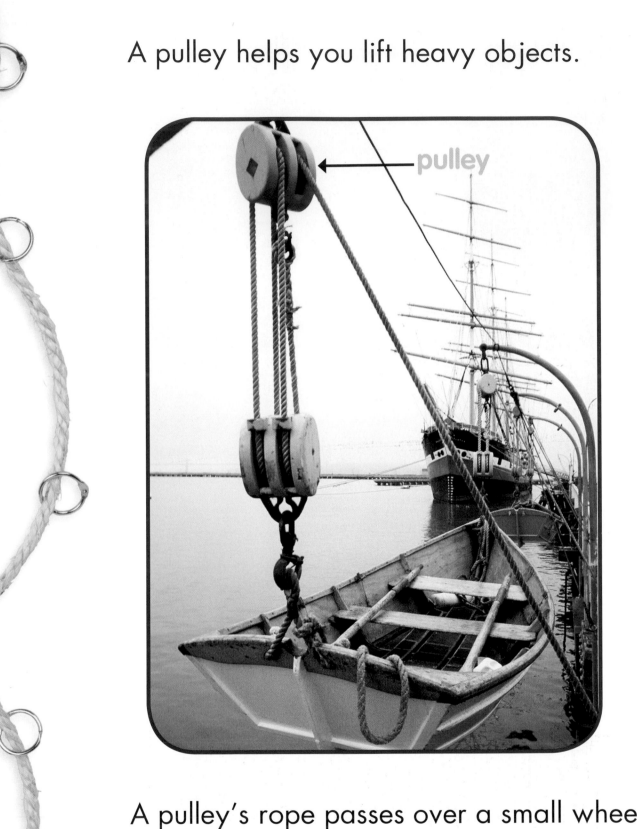

pulley

A pulley's rope passes over a small wheel.
Pull down on one end of the rope. You can lift
a very heavy load tied to the other end.

A pulley can help you raise and lower the flag on a flagpole.

You can even lift the sail on a boat using a pulley.

129

These children are using two kinds of simple machines. A wheelbarrow is a kind of lever, and it has wheels.

Have you used any simple machines today?

131

Think and Share

Talk About It Machines can be very simple. Talk about simple machines you use in the classroom.

1. Use the pictures below to summarize what you learned about machines.

2. What is this selection mostly about?

3. Did you stop to sum up after you read about levers before reading on? How did that help you?

Test Practice

Look Back and Write How would you get an inclined plane to help you get a big box onto a truck? Look back at page 124.

Allan Fowler

Allan Fowler has written many science books for beginning readers. He likes to travel and write about different parts of the world.

Mr. Fowler was born in New York, but he lives in Chicago now. He worked in advertising before he became a writer.

Read more books by Allan Fowler.

133

Roy's Wheelchair

by Collen Watkins

Roy uses a wheelchair. It has axles and wheels. He goes all around town with it.

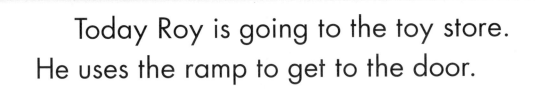

Today Roy is going to the toy store.
He uses the ramp to get to the door.

The door is heavy. He pushes against the opener to get in.

Roy uses his wheelchair to do all kinds of things!

Pronouns

A **pronoun** is a word that takes the place of a noun or nouns. The words **he, she, it, I, we, you,** and **they** are pronouns.

The **boy** uses a ramp.   **He** uses a ramp.

The **girl** climbs
the stairs.   **She** climbs
                                           the stairs.

The **wheel** is round.   **It** is round.

You and I walked.   **We** walked.

Jane, sit down.   **You** sit down.

Chris and Pat lifted it.   **They** lifted it.

Write Using Pronouns

1. Use a pronoun for the words in dark letters. Write the new sentences. Circle the pronouns.

Sara and Mike used a lever.
The lever made the work easier.

· ·

2. Find a sentence in *Simple Machines* that uses a pronoun. Write the sentence. Circle the pronoun.

· ·

3. Write about a simple machine. Use pronouns in some of your sentences. Circle the pronouns.

Let's Talk About
Ideas That Changed the World

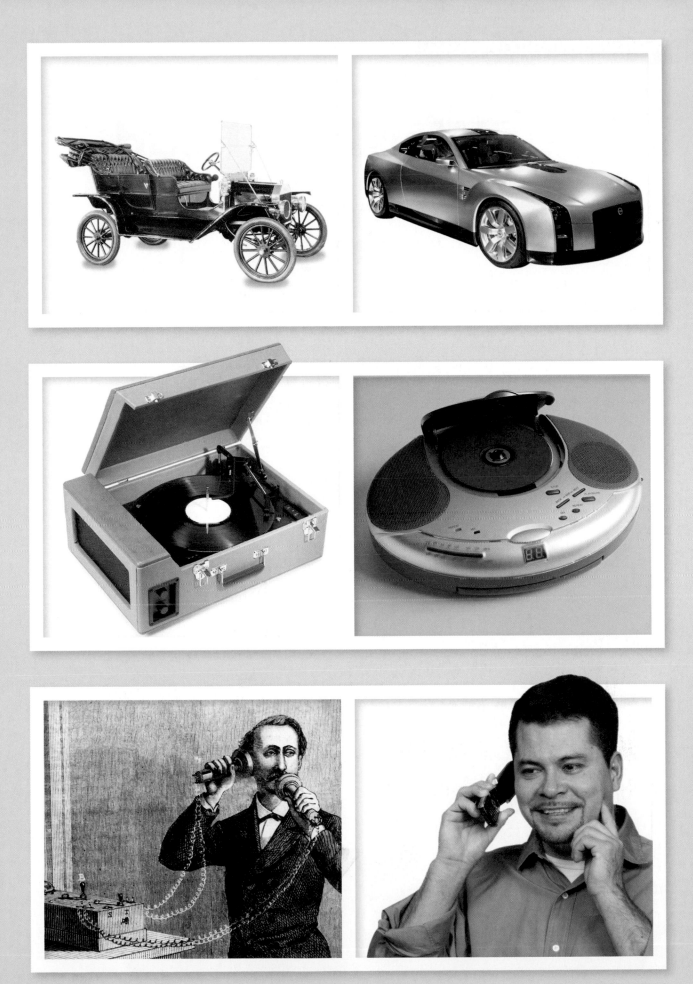

Words to Read

early
learn
science
built
through

Read the Words

Early in life, a man named
Mr. Bell liked to learn about science.
He later built a machine that sent
voices through wires. Do you know
the name of that machine?

Alexander Graham Bell

Genre: Biography
A biography tells a person's life
story. It is written by someone
else. Now you will read about the
man who invented the telephone,
Alexander Graham Bell.

Alexander Graham Bell

by Lola M. Schaefer

Why is Alexander Graham Bell an important person to know?

Alexander Graham Bell was born in Scotland in 1847. His father was a famous teacher who taught people how to speak well.

 **Time line**

born

1847

Scotland

Alexander's mother was deaf. She was still able to teach him to play the piano. Alexander was good at music and science.

 **Time line**

born

1847

**The Bell Family
Alexander is on the left.**

Alexander was interested in
sound. He also liked to invent things.
He built a machine that could speak.
He also tried to make his dog talk.

 # Time line

born

1847

**Alexander using
an early invention**

In 1871, Alexander moved to Boston. During the day, he taught deaf students how to speak. At night, he did experiments with sound.

Time line

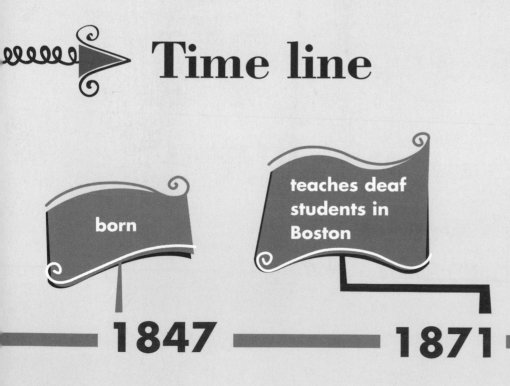

born

teaches deaf students in Boston

1847

1871

**Classroom at a school
for the deaf**

Alexander wanted to learn more about electricity. In 1874, he met Tom Watson. Tom knew how electricity worked. They began to work together.

Time line

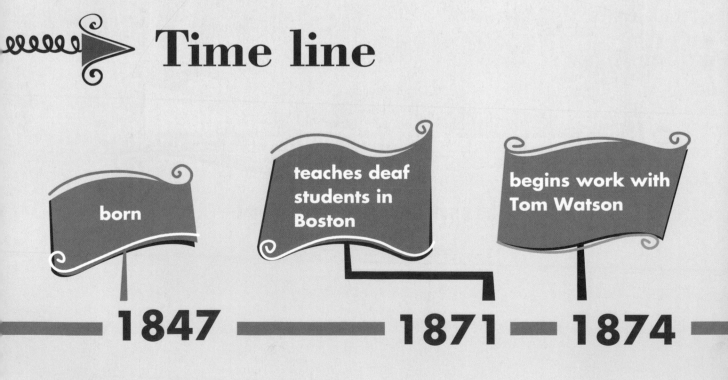

born

teaches deaf students in Boston

begins work with Tom Watson

1847 — **1871** — **1874** —

Electricity can make sound travel through wires.

Alexander stopped teaching. He did experiments day and night. He and Tom wanted to invent a machine that could send voices from one place to another.

Time line

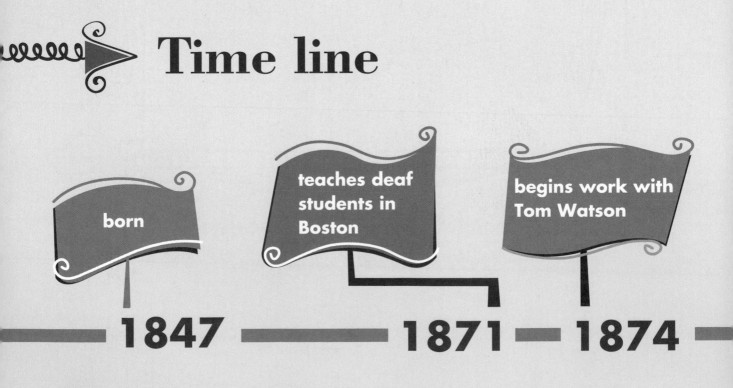

born

teaches deaf students in Boston

begins work with Tom Watson

1847 — **1871** — **1874**

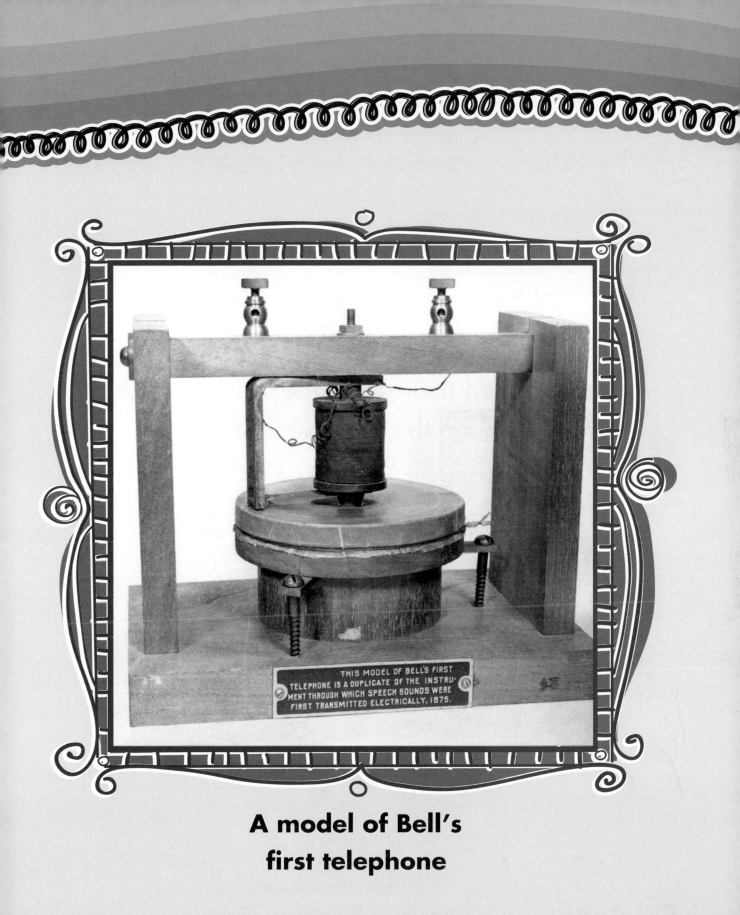

THIS MODEL OF BELL'S FIRST TELEPHONE IS A DUPLICATE OF THE INSTRUMENT THROUGH WHICH SPEECH SOUNDS WERE FIRST TRANSMITTED ELECTRICALLY. 1875.

A model of Bell's first telephone

On March 10, 1876, Alexander and Tom reached their goal. Alexander spoke to Tom through the first telephone.

Time line

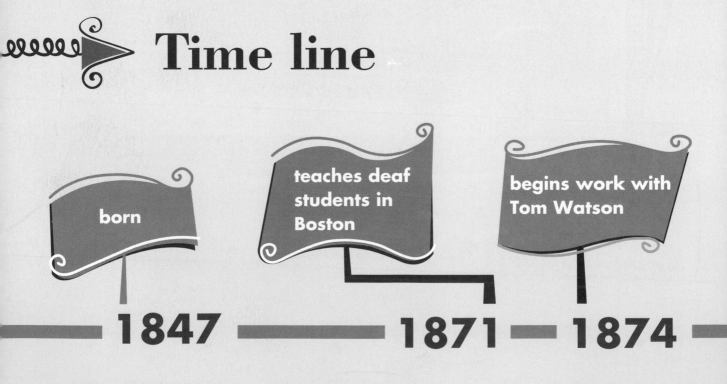

born	teaches deaf students in Boston	begins work with Tom Watson
1847	**1871**	**1874**

Alexander Graham Bell using his telephone

invents telephone with Tom Watson

1876

Alexander and Tom made the telephone better. Soon it could send voices many miles. In 1915, they made the first telephone call across the United States.

Time line

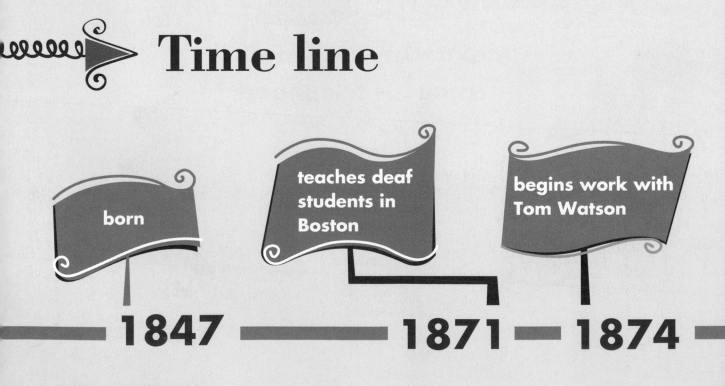

born

teaches deaf students in Boston

begins work with Tom Watson

1847 — 1871 — 1874 —

**The first telephone call
across the United States**

invents
telephone with
Tom Watson

makes first
telephone call
across the
United States

1876 **1915**

Alexander spent his life inventing. He died in 1922. Alexander Graham Bell changed the way people communicate with one another.

Time line

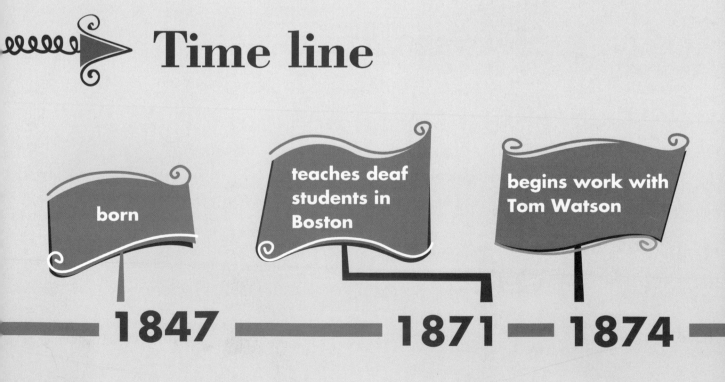

born

teaches deaf students in Boston

begins work with Tom Watson

1847 **1871** **1874**

invents telephone with Tom Watson

makes first telephone call across the United States

dies

1876 — **1915** — **1922**

Read Together

Think and Share

Talk About It What would you say to thank Mr. Alexander Graham Bell for what he did?

1. Use the pictures below to summarize Mr. Bell's life and work.

2. Describe the kind of person Alexander Graham Bell was.

3. How does the time line in this selection help you understand Mr. Bell and his life?

Test Practice

Look Back and Write Look back at page 150. What fantastic thing did Mr. Bell try to do? What do you think happened?

Lola M. Schaefer

As a child, Lola Schaefer loved to read. "I read every biography in our school library," she says. Now she writes biographies for beginning readers.

Ms. Schaefer says, "Whenever you read a good book, pass it to a friend. Then the two of you can talk about your favorite parts."

Read more books by Lola M. Schaefer.

Inventions

THE HISTORY OF INVENTION

Maude likes science. She wants to learn more about inventions. So she visits an Internet Web site called The History of Invention. Here's what she sees.

166

Maude clicks on a picture to learn more.

Sliced bread,
invented in 1928

Maude reads about early inventions like eyeglasses and the first airplane ever built. She learns about inventions all through history—even the invention of sliced bread.

Read Together

Using I and Me

The pronouns **I** and **me** take the place of your name. Use **I** in the subject of a sentence. Use **me** after an action verb. Always write **I** with a capital letter.

I invent things.
My friend helps **me.**

When you talk about yourself and another person, name yourself last. The pronouns **I** and **me** take the place of your name.

Bob and **I** read the instructions.
Ms. Lee helped Bob and **me.**

Write Using I and Me

1. Write these sentences using the correct pronouns.

(I, Me) liked learning about Mr. Bell.
His story gave (I, me) a great idea.
(I, Me) want to invent something.
Jo and (I, me) went to the store.
The teacher helped Jill and (I, me).

· ·

2. Write two sentences that tell what you learned about Alexander Graham Bell. Use the pronouns **I** and **me.**

· ·

3. Write about something you do outside of school. Circle the pronouns **I** and **me.**

169

Let's Talk About Ideas That Changed the World

Words to Read

brothers
answered
poor
carry
different

172

Read the Words

"How many brothers did Ben Franklin have?" asked Kenji.

"I don't know," answered Carlos, "but I read that his family was poor."

"He liked to carry out many different experiments," added Kate.

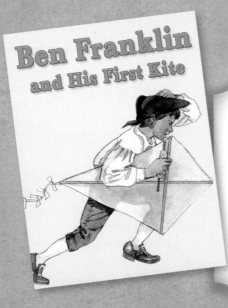

Genre: Biography
A biography sometimes tells about only a small part of a person's life. Next you will read about Ben Franklin when he was a boy.

Ben Franklin
and His First Kite

written by Stephen Krensky

illustrated by Bert Dodson

What will Ben do
with his kite?

Ten-year-old Benjamin Franklin was hard at work in his father's candle shop. He was cutting wicks. He carefully laid out each one.

Ben stretched his arms and let out a yawn. Candles could be tall or short, fat or thin, and even different colors. But there was nothing fun about candles for Ben.

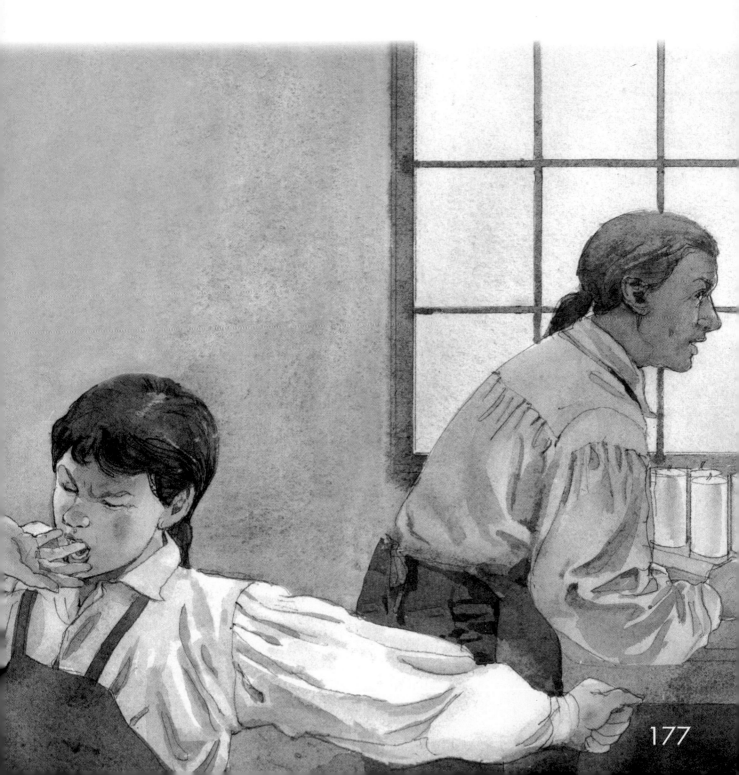

"When do you think we'll be done today?"
Ben asked his father.

"Soon enough," his father answered.
"Why? Do you have special plans?"

Ben's father smiled. It was a rare day indeed when Ben did not have a plan in mind.

"Yes," said Ben. "I want to try an experiment at the millpond."

"You'll be swimming, then?" his father asked.

Ben grinned. "Partly," he said.

His father nodded. Ben was a fine swimmer.

That afternoon Ben flew down the streets of Boston. He was headed for home. Along the way he noticed the waves cresting in the harbor. The ships rocked back and forth. That was good, he thought. He needed a strong wind today.

When Ben got to his house, his mother met him at the door. Inside, two of his sisters were busy making hasty pudding by the hearth. Ben had sixteen brothers and sisters.

"Ben," his mother said, "why are you in such a hurry?"

Ben told her about his plan.

"Since your father approves, I won't keep you," said his mother. "Just be back for supper."

Ben nodded. He ran to get the kite he had made the week before. Then he left the house.

At the millpond a few of Ben's friends had arrived to watch.

"You've picked a poor place to fly a kite," said one.

Ben shrugged. "I'm doing an experiment," he said.

Ben got undressed. He gave his clothes to one of his friends.

"Please carry these to the other side of the pond," he said.

"What are you going to do?" asked the other boys. "Carry the kite while you swim?"

"No," said Ben. "The kite is going to carry me."

"But that kite is nothing special. It's just paper, sticks, and string," said one boy.

"That's true," Ben said. "But you see, the kite isn't the invention. The invention is what I'm going to do with it."

Ben raised the kite in the air. Once the wind had caught and carried it aloft, Ben walked into the water. There he lay on his back, floating.

"I'm going to cross this pond without swimming a stroke," said Ben.

The wind tugged on the kite. The kite string tightened. The water began to ripple at Ben's feet. The kite was pulling him!

The boys whooped and hollered
as Ben glided across the pond. Finally
he reached the other side. The other
boys met him there.

"That was amazing!" said one.

"You crossed the whole pond without
swimming a stroke," said another.

"What will you do next?" they asked.
"Another invention? A different experiment?"
Ben didn't know. But he was sure he would think of something.

Ben's Great

Ben Franklin

Benjamin Franklin proved that lightning is electricity.

Franklin invented lightning rods. They are put on houses to prevent fires caused by lightning.

Ideas

Chair with ladder

Bifocal glasses

Franklin stove

Think and Share

Talk About It Would you like to have been a friend of Ben Franklin's? Explain.

1. Decide in which order the pictures belong. Use them to retell Ben's story.

2 What did you learn about great ideas from reading this biography?

3. What questions did you ask yourself as you read this selection? How did that help you with your reading?

Look Back and Write Why was a strong wind important to Ben on this day? Look back at page 189 to help you answer.

196

Stephen Krensky

Stephen Krensky is the author of over seventy books for children! He says, "Writing is hard and fun at the same time."

As a boy Mr. Krensky liked to make up stories. He would pretend he was in big adventures. Today he lives in Massachusetts with his wife and two sons, Andrew and Peter.

Read more books by Stephen Krensky.

I Made a Mechanical Dragon

by Jack Prelutsky
illustrated by Peter Sis

I made a mechanical dragon
Of bottle tops, hinges, and strings,
Of thrown-away clocks and unmendable socks,
Of hangers and worn innersprings.
I built it of cardboard and plastic,
Of doorknobs and cables and corks,
Of spools and balloons and unusable spoons,
And rusty old hinges and forks.

It's quite an unusual dragon
It rolls on irregular wheels,
It clatters and creaks and it rattles and squeaks,
And when it tips over, it squeals.
I've tried to control its maneuvers,
It fails to obey my commands,
It bumps into walls till it totters and falls—
I made it myself with my hands!

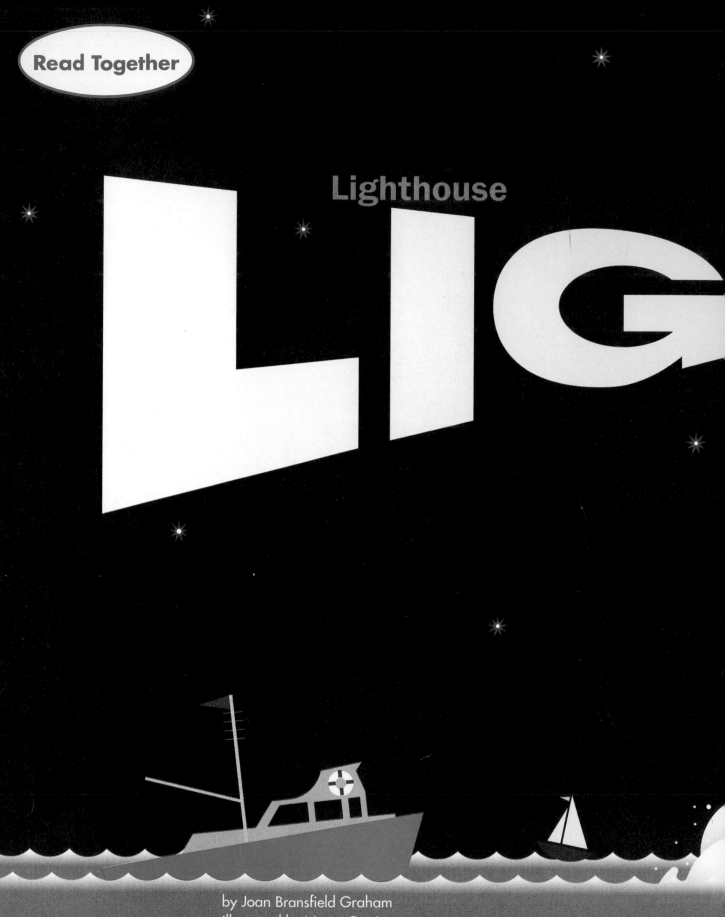

Lighthouse

LIG

by Joan Bransfield Graham
illustrated by Nancy Davis

Oh, Captain of the midnight sky, you stretch your arms and flash your eye across the waves and churning foam to steer me, guide me, safely HOME.

LIGHT HOUSE

More About Pronouns

A **pronoun** can take the place of some words in a sentence. **I, you, he, she, it, we,** and **they** are used in the **naming part** of a sentence. **Me, you, him, her, it, us,** and **them** are used in the **action part**.

Ben had a kite.   **He** had a kite.

The work was done.   **It** was done.

His friends helped him.   **They** helped him.

They like **Ben**.   They like **him**.

Ben called **his mother**.   Ben called **her**.

Ben saw **Tom and Meg**.   Ben saw **them**.

Write Using More Pronouns

1. Write these sentences. Use pronouns in place of the words in dark letters.

Ben crossed the pond
The wind blew him across.
Ben surprised **his friends**.

. . . .

2. Find two sentences in *Ben Franklin and His First Kite* that use pronouns. Write the sentences. Circle the pronouns.

. . . .

3. Write sentences about an experiment or a project that you did with your friends. Use pronouns. Circle them.

Wrap-Up

What's the Big Idea?

connect to WRITING

Look around your home and school. Find a machine or another idea that makes a big difference in your life. Draw a picture of it. Write how it changes your life.

What difference can a great idea make?

The Best Idea

What was the best idea you read about in this unit? Choose the story that tells about the best idea. Act out the story with a friend. Tell how the idea makes a difference.

A Good Result

connect to SOCIAL STUDIES

Mole did not want his bird to fly. Then Grandad changed Mole's mind. Think about a time you changed your mind. Why was that a good idea? Talk it over with a partner.

100%

☺ YES!

I Can Find the Answer

Where can you find the answers to questions?

Right There  **In the Book**

Sometimes the answers are RIGHT THERE in the book. You can put your finger right on the answer.

You might read this text and this question:

Hurray! Today is the 4th of July. My family will go to a party on our block. At night we ← will see fireworks. They will light up the dark sky.

1 **When will the family see fireworks?**

○ in the morning

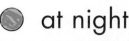 at night

○ the next day

 Look back at the text.
The answer is RIGHT THERE.

I Can Find the Answer

In My Head

Sometimes the answers are NOT right there in the text. You must read what the author wrote and use your head. You must FIGURE IT OUT!

You might read this text and this question:

We all went to the park to see the fireworks. Crack! Bang! The sounds were very loud. Then a baby began to cry. She cried very hard!

1 **How did the baby feel?**

○ happy

○ cold

◉ afraid

Look at this clue. You can use your head to FIGURE OUT how the baby feels.

Try It! ⬤ ○ ○

In the Book

Sometimes the answers are RIGHT THERE in the book. You can put your finger right on the answer.

You might read this text and this question:

Mr. Bear liked lots of foods. He liked to eat bugs. He liked to eat grass. But Mr. Bear's favorite treat was honey.

1 **What did Mr. Bear like most?**

○ bugs

○ grass

○ honey

Look back at the text.
The answer is RIGHT THERE.

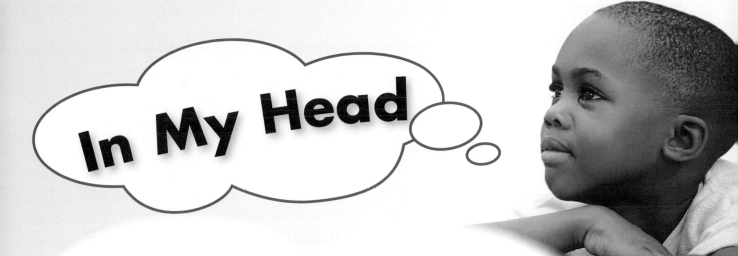

In My Head

Sometimes the answers are NOT right there in the text. You must read the text and use your head to find the answers. You must FIGURE IT OUT!

You might read this text and this question:

Mr. Bear was looking for food. He saw bees flying into a hive. "Yes!" said Mr. Bear. He knew something good was inside the hive. Soon he would eat a good dinner.

1 **What will Mr. Bear have for dinner?**

- ○ bees
- ○ hive
- ○ honey

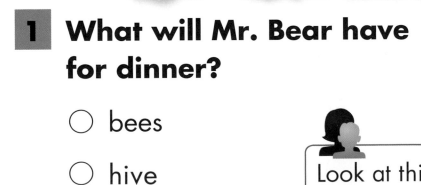

Look at this clue. It will help you choose the right answer.

Glossary

Aa

amazing Something that is **amazing** is very surprising. The hero made an **amazing** escape.

axles **Axles** are bars on which wheels turn.

axle

Bb

borrowed If you **borrowed** something, you got it from a person or a place just for a while. I **borrowed** books from the library.

Boston **Boston** is the capital city of Massachusetts, which is a state in the United States.

210

breath **Breath** is air taken into and sent out of the lungs. Take a deep **breath.**

Cc

communicate To **communicate** is to give and take news and information.

Dd

detectives **Detectives** are police officers or other people who work at solving mysteries.

disagreed If you and a friend **disagreed,** that means both had different ideas.

disagreed

Ee

electricity **Electricity** is a kind of energy that makes light and heat. **Electricity** also runs motors. **Electricity** makes light bulbs shine, radios and televisions play, and cars start.

Ff

famous A **famous** person is one who is well-known and important. The **famous** singer was met by a large crowd.

favorite Your **favorite** thing is the one you like better than all the others. What is your **favorite** flower?

Hh

harbor A **harbor** is an area of water where ships are safe. The boat sailed for the **harbor** when the storm began.

harbor

hearth

hasty pudding **Hasty pudding** is mush made of cornmeal.

hearth A **hearth** is the stone or brick floor of a fireplace.

hey **Hey** is a sound you make to get someone's attention.

hurray **Hurray** is what you shout when you are very happy. Give a **hurray** for our team!

Ii

inclined plane An **inclined plane** is a plank or other flat surface placed at an angle and used to move heavy things to a higher place. It is a simple machine.

inclined plane

invention An **invention** is a new thing that someone makes or thinks of. The light bulb was a wonderful **invention.**

Ll

lawn A **lawn** is a piece of land that is covered with grass and near a house. The grass of a **lawn** is usually kept short.

Mm

machines **Machines** are things with moving parts that do work for you. Cars, washers, and computers are **machines.**

meadow A **meadow** is a piece of land where grass grows. There are sheep in the **meadow.**

meadow

million A **million** is a very large number. It is also written 1,000,000.

mystery A **mystery** is something that is hard to understand. It was a **mystery** why the radio started playing in the middle of the night.

215

Pp

piano A **piano** is a large musical instrument that you sit at and play with your fingers.

potato bug

potato bugs **Potato bugs** are beetles that eat the leaves of the potato plant.

presently **Presently** means at the present time, or now. She is **presently** in first grade.

pulleys **Pulleys** are wheels with ropes that help lift things.

pulley

Ss

Scotland **Scotland** is a country north of England.

solve When you **solve** something, you find the answer to it. The detective will **solve** the mystery by using the clues.

solved **Solved** is the past tense of *solve*.

surface A **surface** is the top part or outside of something. The **surface** of the road was very wet after the rain.

surface

Tt

telephone A **telephone** is something you use to talk to people far away. Please answer the **telephone** if it rings.

telephone

tippy-toe **Tippy-toe** means on the tips of your toes. The girl walked **tippy-toe** so that she would not wake her baby brother.

tippy-toe

218

Uu   **usually** If something **usually** happens, it happens very often or almost all the time. We **usually** eat dinner at six o'clock.

Vv   **vacuum** A **vacuum** cleaner is a machine you can use to clean rugs, curtains, and floors.

vacuum

Tested Words

Tippy-Toe Chick, Go!

along
behind
eyes
never
pulling
toward

Mole and the Baby Bird

door
loved
should
wood

Dot & Jabber and the
Great Acorn Mystery

among
another
instead
none

Simple Machines

against
goes
heavy
kinds
today

Tested Words

Alexander Graham Bell

built
early
learn
science
through

Ben Franklin and His First Kite

answered
brothers
carry
different
poor

Acknowledgments

Text

Page 14: *Tippy-Toe Chick, Go!* by George Shannon, illustrations by Laura Dronzek. Text copyright © 2003 by George W. B. Shannon. Illustrations copyright © 2003 by Laura Dronzek. Used by permission of HarperCollins Publishers.

Page 48: *Mole and the Baby Bird* by Marjorie Newman, illustrated by Patrick Benson. Text copyright © 2002 by Marjorie Newman. Illustrations copyright © 2002 by Patrick Benson. Reprinted by permission of Bloomsbury Publishing.

Page 80: Excerpt from *Dot & Jabber and the Great Acorn Mystery*, copyright © 2001 by Ellen Stoll Walsh, reprinted by permission of Harcourt, Inc. This material may not be reproduced in any form or by any means without the prior written permission of the publisher.

Page 114: From *Simple Machines* by Allan Fowler. © 2001 Children's Press®. A Division of Grolier Publishing Co., Inc. All rights reserved. Published simultaneously in Canada. Reprinted by permission.

Page 144: *Alexander Graham Bell* by Lola M. Schaefer. Copyright © 2003 by Capstone Press. Reprinted by permission.

Page 174: From *Ben Franklin and His First Kite*. Text copyright © 2002 by Stephen Krensky. Illustrations copyright © 2002 by Bert Dodson. Reprinted with permission of Aladdin Paperbacks, Simon & Schuster Children's Publishing Division. All rights reserved.

Page 198: "I Made A Mechanical Dragon" from *The Dragons are Singing Tonight* by Jack Prelutsky, illustrated by Peter Sis. Text copyright © 1993 by Jack Prelutsky. Illustrations copyright © 1993 by Peter Sis. Used by permission of HarperCollins Publishers.

Page 200: "Lighthouse" from *Flicker Flash*. Text copyright © 1999 by Joan Bransfield Graham. Illustrations copyright © 1999 by Nancy Davis. Reprinted by permission of Houghton Mifflin Company. All rights reserved.

Illustrations

Cover: Daniel Moreton

14-33 Laura Dronzek

36-41 Viviana Garofoli

44-73 Patrick Benson

198 Peter Sis

Photographs

Every effort has been made to secure permission and provide appropriate credit for photographic material. The publisher deeply regrets any omission and pledges to correct errors called to its attention in subsequent editions.

Unless otherwise acknowledged, all photographs are the property of Scott Foresman, a division of Pearson Education.

Photo locators denoted as follows: Top (T), Center (C), Bottom (B), Left (L), Right (R), Background (Bkgd).

7 ©Xavier Bonghi/Getty Images

8 (Bkgd) ©Bill Ross/Corbis, (L) ©Xavier Bonghi/Getty Images

9 (CR) ©Ross Whitaker/Getty Images, (BR) ©Bettmann/Corbis

10 ©Andy Roberts/Stone/Getty Images

11 (BL) Getty Images, (T) Ghislain & Marie David de Lossy/Image Bank/Getty Images

44 ©Martin Harvey/Gallo Images/Corbis

45 (TL, BL) AP/Wide World Photos, (CR) ©Chinch Grynicwicz/Ecoscene/Corbis

103 ©Benjamin M. Walsh

110 ©Peter Samuels/Corbis

111 (B) ©Dennis MacDonald/PhotoEdit, (T) ©Royalty-Free/Corbis, (CR) ©Derek P. Redfearn/Getty Images

112 Getty Images

113 ©Comstock, Inc.

114 (CL) ©Comstock, Inc., (BC) Corbis

115 (Bkgd) ©Ross Whitaker/Getty Images, (BC) ©Comstock, Inc.

116 (CR) Corbis, (B) ©Comstock, Inc.

117 ©Nance S. Trueworthy

119 ©Tony Freeman/PhotoEdit

120 ©Michelle D. Bridwell/PhotoEdit

122 (TR) ©Royalty-Free/Corbis, (TL) ©Kayte M. Deioma/PhotoEdit, (B) ©Dennis MacDonald/PhotoEdit

123 Stock Boston

124 (T) ©David Young-Wolff/PhotoEdit, (B) ©Bonnie Kamin/PhotoEdit

125 ©David Forbert/SuperStock

126 Unicorn Stock Photos

Acknowledgments

127 (T) Affordable Photo Stock/Francis & Donna Caldwell, (B) ©Royalty-Free/Corbis

128 Stock Boston

129 (TL) ©Mary Kate Denny/PhotoEdit, (BR) ©Laurence Monneret/Getty Images

130 Stock Boston

131 (TL, BR) ©Tom Stewart/Corbis, (TR) ©Jennie Woodcock/Reflections Photolibrary/Corbis, (BL) ©George Shelley/Corbis

133 ©Comstock, Inc.

139 ©David Forbert/SuperStock

140 ©Royalty-Free/Corbis

141 (BL, TL) ©Bettmann/Corbis, (TR) Reuters/Corbis

142 ©Bettmann/Corbis

145 Corbis

147 ©E.O. Hoppe

149 ©A. G. Bell National Historic Site

151 ©Bettmann/Corbis

153 Corbis

155 ©Gordon Osmundson/Corbis

157, 159, 161 ©Bettmann/Corbis

163 Corbis

166 (L, CC, CL) Hemera Technologies, (CR) Wright State University Library

167 Hemera Technologies

169 Corbis

170 ©Ariel Skelley/Corbis

171 (Bkgd) ©ML Sinibaldi/Corbis, (BL) Terry W. Eggers/Corbis, (TR) ©Jennie Woodcock/Corbis, (C) ©Richard Cummins/Corbis

194 (TL) ©Stock Montage/SuperStock, (BL) North Wind Picture Archives, (CR) The Granger Collection, NY

195 (CL) ©Bettmann/Corbis, (B) The Granger Collection, NY, (TR) ©Jeff Greenberg

197 ©Stephen Krensky

204 (CL) ©David Young-Wolff/PhotoEdit, (BL) ©Xavier Bonghi/Getty Images, (Bkgd) ©Bill Ross/Corbis

207, 209 ©Larry Williams/Corbis

209 ©Larry Williams/Corbis

210 Unicorn Stock Photos

211 ©Ariel Skelley/Corbis

213 (TR, CL) Getty Images

214 ©David Young-Wolff/PhotoEdit

215 Getty Images

216 (BR) Stock Boston, (CL) ©Royalty-Free/Corbis

217 ©Royalty-Free/Corbis

218 Getty Images

219 Corbis

221 ©Nance S. Trueworthy

222 ©Bettmann/Corbis

Glossary

The contents of this glossary have been adapted from *First Dictionary*. Copyright © 2000, Pearson Education, Inc.

Indiana

Academic Standards

Grade 1

Standard 1

READING: Word Recognition, Fluency, and Vocabulary Development

Students understand the basic features of words. They see letter patterns and know how to translate them into spoken language by using phonics (an understanding of the different letters that make different sounds), syllables, and word parts (-s, -ed, -ing). They apply this knowledge to achieve fluent (smooth and clear) oral and silent reading. They listen to stories read aloud to them and use the vocabulary in those stories in their oral language.

Concepts About Print

1.1.1   Match oral words to printed words.

1.1.2   Identify letters, words, and sentences.

1.1.3   Recognize that sentences start with capital letters and end with punctuation, such as periods, question marks, and exclamation points.

Phonemic Awareness

1.1.4   Distinguish beginning, middle, and ending sounds in single-syllable words (words with only one vowel sound).
Example: Tell the sound that comes at the beginning of the word *sun*. Tell the sound that comes at the end of the word *cloud*. Tell the sound that comes in the middle of the word *boat*.

1.1.5   Recognize different vowel sounds in orally stated single-syllable words.
Example: Say the sound that is in the middle of the word *bit*. Say the sound that is in the middle of the word *bite*. Tell whether this is the same sound or a different sound.

1.1.6   Recognize that vowels' sounds can be represented by different letters.

1.1.7   Create and state a series of rhyming words.

1.1.8   Add, delete, or change sounds to change words.
Example: Tell what letter you would have to change to make the word *cow* into the word *how*. Tell what letter you would have to change to make the word *pan* into *an*.

1.1.8.A1   Identify important signs and symbols, such as stop signs or school crossing signs or restroom symbols, from the colors, shapes, logos, and letters on the signs or symbols.

1.1.9   Blend two-to-four phonemes (sounds) into recognizable words.
Example: Tell what word is made by the sounds /b/ /a/ /t/. Tell what word is made by the sounds /fl/ /a/ /t/.

Decoding and Word Recognition

1.1.10   Generate the sounds from all the letters and from a variety of letter patterns, including consonant blends and long- and short-vowel patterns (*a, e, i, o, u*), and blend those sounds into recognizable words.

1.1.11   Read common sight words (words that are often seen and heard).

1.1.12   Use phonic and context clues as self-correction strategies when reading.

1.1.13   Read words by using knowledge of vowel digraphs (two vowels that make one sound such as the *ea* in *eat*) and knowledge of how vowel sounds change when followed by the letter *r* (such as the *ea* in the word *ear*).
Example: Correctly read aloud the vowel sounds made in words, such as *ear, eat, near, their,* or *wear*.

1.1.14   Read common word patterns (*-ite, -ate*).
Example: Read words, such as *gate, late,* and *kite*.

1.1.15   Read aloud smoothly and easily in familiar text.

Vocabulary and Concept Development

1.1.16   Read and understand simple compound words (*birthday, anything*) and contractions (*isn't, aren't, can't, won't*).

1.1.17   Read and understand root words (*look*) and their inflectional forms (*looks, looked, looking*).
Example: Recognize that the *s* added to the end of *chair* makes it mean more than one chair. Recognize that adding *ed* to the end of *jump* makes it mean jumping that happened in the past.

1.1.18   Classify categories of words.
Example: Tell which of the following are fruits and which are vegetables: bananas, oranges, apples, carrots, and peas.

1.1.18.A1   Listen to stories read aloud and use the vocabulary in those stories in oral language.

Standard 2

READING: Comprehension and Analysis of Nonfiction and Informational Text

Students read and understand grade-level-appropriate material. They use a variety of comprehension strategies, such as asking and responding to essential questions, drawing conclusions, making predictions, and comparing information from several sources, to understand what they read. The selections in the **Indiana Reading List** *(available online at www.doe.state.in.us/standards/readinglist.html) illustrate the quality and complexity of the materials to be read by students. In addition to their regular school reading, at Grade 1, students begin to read a variety of grade-level-appropriate nonfiction and informational texts, such as alphabet books, picture books or books on science, social studies, mathematics and other subjects, children's magazines and periodicals, beginners' dictionaries, and online information.*

Structural Features of Nonfiction and Informational Materials

1.2.1   Identify the title, author, illustrator, and table of contents of a reading selection.

1.2.1.A1   Locate age-and-content appropriate information online with the aid of a teacher or educator.

Analysis of Grade-Level-Appropriate Text

1.2.2   Identify text that uses sequence (*first, second, third*) or other logical order (alphabetical order or time).
Example: Explain how an informational text is different from a story.
Tell what might be included in an informational book that uses sequence, such as a book on making a bird feeder like *The Bird Table* by Pauline Cartwright.

1.2.3   Respond to *who, what, when, where, why,* and *how* questions and discuss the main idea of what is read.
Example: Read a story, such as *Frog and Toad Together* by Arnold Lobel or *There's an Alligator Under My Bed* by Mercer Mayer, and tell about the story, including the main idea, important events *(what, when, why, how)*, setting *(where)*, and characters *(who)*.

1.2.4   Follow one-step written instructions.

1.2.5   Use context (the meaning of the surrounding text) to understand word and sentence meanings.

1.2.6   Draw conclusions or confirm predictions about what will happen next in a text by identifying key words (signal words that alert the reader to a sequence of events, such as *before, first, during, while, as, at the same time, after, then, next, at last, finally, now, when,* or cause-and-effect, such as *because, since, therefore, so*).

1.2.7   Relate prior knowledge to what is read.

READING: Comprehension, Literary Response, and Analysis of Fiction

Students read and respond to a wide variety of children's literature. They use comprehension strategies, such as identifying and discussing the characters, theme (the main message of a story), plot (what happens in a story), and setting (where a story takes place) of stories that they read. The selections in the **Indiana Reading List** *(available online at www.doe.state.in.us/standards/readinglist.html) illustrate the quality and complexity of the materials to be read by students. At Grade 1, students begin to read a wide variety of fiction, such as classic and contemporary literature, folk tales, poetry or songs, plays, and others.*

Literary Analysis of Grade-Level-Appropriate Text

1.3.1   Identify and describe the plot, setting, or character(s) in a story. Retell a story's beginning, middle, and ending.
Example: Read a story, such as *Arthur's Prize Reader* by Lillian Hoban. Retell the story, including descriptions of the characters and plot of the story, by telling about what happens to Arthur in the contest that he enters and the one that he helps his sister to enter. Plot the story onto a story map.

1.3.1.A1   Confirm predictions about what will happen next in a story.
Example: Read part of a story, such as *The Musicians of Bremen: A Tale from Germany* by Jane Yolen, and tell what might happen next and how the story might end.

1.3.2   Describe the roles of authors and illustrators.
Example: Read a book, such as *The Very Hungry Caterpillar* by Eric Carle or *Where the Wild Things Are* by Maurice Sendak, in which the art is especially important in telling the story. Describe the different roles of the author and illustrator, and discuss how the pictures help to tell the story.

1.3.2.A1   Distinguish fantasy from reality.

1.3.2.A2   Understand what is read or heard by responding to questions *(who, what, when, where, why, how)* and by using other appropriate comprehension strategies from Standard 2 such as responding to questions about conclusions, context, prior knowledge, or sequence.

WRITING: Process

Students discuss ideas for group stories and other writing. Students write clear sentences and paragraphs that develop a central idea. Students progress through the stages of the writing process, including prewriting, drafting, revising, and editing multiple drafts.

Organization and Focus

1.4.1   Discuss ideas and select a focus for group stories or other writing.

1.4.2   Use various organizational strategies to plan writing.

Evaluation and Revision

1.4.3   Revise writing for others to read.

WRITING: Applications (Different Types of Writing and Their Characteristics)

At Grade 1, students begin to write compositions that describe and explain familiar objects, events, and experiences. Students use their understanding of the sounds of words to write simple rhymes. Student writing demonstrates a command of Standard English and the drafting, research, and organizational strategies outlined in Standard 4 — Writing Process. Writing demonstrates an awareness of the audience (intended reader) and purpose for writing.

Using the writing strategies of Grade 1 outlined in Standard 4 — Writing Process, students:

1.5.1   Write brief narratives (stories) describing an experience.
Example: Write a short story titled *My Friend* describing an experience that is real or imagined.

1.5.2   Write brief expository (informational) descriptions of a real object, person, place, or event, using sensory details.
Example: Write a description of a family member, a pet, or a favorite toy. Include enough details that the reader can picture the person, animal, or object.

1.5.3   Write simple rhymes.

1.5.4   Use descriptive words when writing.
Example: Use varied words to describe events, people, and places, such as describing a day as a *sunny day* or *cloudy day*.

1.5.5   Write for different purposes and to a specific audience or person.
Example: Write a thank-you note to the store manager after a field trip to the local supermarket.

WRITING: English Language Conventions

Students write using Standard English conventions appropriate to this grade level.

Handwriting

1.6.1   Print legibly and space letters, words, and sentences appropriately.

Sentence Structure

1.6.2   Write in complete sentences.

Grammar

1.6.3   Identify and correctly use singular and plural nouns *(dog/dogs)*.

1.6.4   Identify and correctly write contractions *(isn't, aren't, can't)*.

1.6.5   Identify and correctly write possessive nouns *(cat's meow, girls' dresses)* and possessive pronouns *(my/mine, his/hers)*.

Punctuation

1.6.6   Correctly use periods *(I am five.)*, exclamation points *(Help!)*, and question marks *(How old are you?)* at the end of sentences.

Capitalization

1.6.7   Capitalize the first word of a sentence, names of people, and the pronoun *I*.

Spelling

1.6.8   Spell correctly three- and four-letter words *(can, will)* and grade-level-appropriate sight words *(red, fish)*.

LISTENING AND SPEAKING: Skills, Strategies, and Applications

Students listen critically and respond appropriately to oral communication. They speak in a manner that guides the listener to understand important ideas by using proper phrasing, pitch, and modulation (raising and lowering voice). Students deliver brief oral presentations about familiar experiences or interests that are organized around a coherent thesis statement (a statement of topic). Students use the same Standard English conventions for oral speech that they use in their writing.

Comprehension

1.7.1   Listen attentively.

1.7.2   Ask questions for clarification and understanding.

1.7.3   Give, restate, and follow simple two-step directions.

Organization and Delivery of Oral Communication

1.7.4   Stay on the topic when speaking.

1.7.5   Use descriptive words when speaking about people, places, things, and events.

Speaking Applications

1.7.6   Recite poems, rhymes, songs, and stories.

1.7.7   Retell stories using basic story grammar and relating the sequence of story events by answering *who, what, when, where, why,* and *how* questions.

1.7.8   Relate an important life event or personal experience in a simple sequence.

1.7.9   Provide descriptions with careful attention to sensory detail.

1.7.10   Use visual aids, such as pictures and objects, to present oral information.

Looking Back: GRADE K

Indiana

English/Language Arts

Academic Standards

Standard 1

READING: Word Recognition, Fluency, and Vocabulary Development

Students know about letters, words, and sounds. They apply this knowledge to read simple sentences. They listen to stories read aloud to them and use the vocabulary in those stories in their oral language.

Concepts About Print

K.1.1   Identify the front cover, back cover, and title page of a book.

K.1.2   Follow words from left to right and from top to bottom on the printed page.

K.1.3   Understand that printed materials provide information.

K.1.4   Recognize that sentences in print are made up of separate words.

K.1.5   Distinguish letters from words.

K.1.6   Recognize and name all capital and lowercase letters of the alphabet.

Phonemic Awareness*

K.1.7   Listen to two or three phonemes (sounds) when they are read aloud, and tell the number of sounds heard, whether they are the same or different, and the order. Example: Listen to the sounds /f/, /m/, /s/ or /l/, /n/, /v/. Tell how many sounds were heard and whether any sounds were the same.

K.1.8   Listen and say the changes in spoken syllables (a word or part of a word that contains one vowel sound) and words with two or three sounds when one sound is added, substituted, omitted, moved, or repeated. Example: Listen to the word *bat* and tell what word is left when you take the /b/ sound away. Tell what word is left when you take the /br/ sound away from the spoken word *brother*.

K.1.9   Blend consonant-vowel-consonant (cvc) sounds aloud to make words.
Example: Listen to the sounds /b/, /e/, /d/ and tell what word is made.

K.1.10   Say rhyming words in response to an oral prompt.
Example: Say a word that rhymes with *cat*.

K.1.11   Listen to one-syllable words and tell the beginning or ending sounds.
Example: Tell what sound you hear at the beginning of the word *girl*.

K.1.12   Listen to spoken sentences and recognize individual words in the sentence;
listen to words and recognize individual sounds in the words.

K.1.13   Count the number of sounds in a syllable; count the number of syllables
in words.

*When letters have a slanted line before and after them, such as /f/, /sh/, /b/, this
represents the sound the letter makes, not the name of the letter.

Decoding and Word Recognition

K.1.14   Match all consonant sounds (*mad, red, pin, top, sun*) to appropriate letters.

K.1.15   Read one-syllable and high-frequency (often-heard) words by sight.

K.1.16   Use self-correcting strategies when reading simple sentences.

K.1.17   Read their own names.

K.1.18   Understand the alphabetic principle, which means that as letters in words
change, so do the sounds.

K.1.19   Learn and apply knowledge of alphabetical order (first letter) when using a
classroom or school library/media center.

Vocabulary and Concept Development

K.1.20   Identify and sort common words in basic categories.
Example: Tell whether the words *blue, yellow,* and *red* are colors, shapes, or
foods. Tell the names of some favorite colors.

K.1.21   Identify common signs and symbols.
Example: Identify the meanings of common signs and symbols, such as stop
signs or store signs, from the colors, shapes, logos, and letters on these signs
or symbols.

K.1.21.A1   Listen to stories read aloud and use the vocabulary in those stories in
oral language.

Standard
2

READING: Comprehension and Analysis of Nonfiction and Informational Text

*Students identify the basic facts and ideas in what they have read, heard, or seen.
They use comprehension strategies, such as generating and responding to questions
and comparing new information to what is already known, to understand what they
read. The selections in the **Indiana Reading List** (www.doe.state.in.us/standards/
readinglist.html) illustrate the quality and complexity of the materials to be read
by students. In Kindergarten, students will listen to and begin to read grade- level-
appropriate nonfiction and informational texts, such as alphabet books, picture books
on science, social studies, mathematics, and other subjects, beginners' dictionaries,
and online information.*

Structural Features of Informational and Technical Materials

K.2.1　　Locate the title and the name of the author of a book.

K.2.1.A1　Locate age-and-content-appropriate information online with the aid of a teacher or educator.

Analysis of Grade-Level-Appropriate Nonfiction and Informational Text

K.2.2　　Use picture and context clues to aid comprehension and to draw conclusions or make predictions.

K.2.3　　Connect the information or events in texts to prior knowledge or life experiences.

K.2.4　　Identify types of everyday print materials.
　　　　　　Example: Walk around the school and identify the signs in the school, such as EXIT, Principal's Office, and Restrooms. Tell the difference between a storybook and a beginners' dictionary.

K.2.5　　Identify and discuss the main ideas or put the information in order (*first, next,* and *then*).

K.2.5.A1　Use the comprehension strategy of generating and responding to questions (*who, what, when, where, why, how*).

READING: Comprehension, Literary Response, and Analysis of Fiction

Students listen and respond to stories based on well-known characters, themes (the main message of a story), plots (what happens in a story), and settings (where a story takes place). They use comprehension strategies, such as recognizing the difference between fantasy and reality and retelling stories (beginning, middle, end), to understand what they read. The selections in the **Indiana Reading List** *(www. doe.state.in.us/standards/readinglist.html) illustrate the quality and complexity of the materials to be read by students. In Kindergarten, students will listen and respond to grade-level-appropriate fiction, such as classic and contemporary literature, nursery rhymes or songs, folk tales, plays, and others.*

Literary Analysis of Grade-Level-Appropriate Narratives (Stories)

K.3.1　　Distinguish fantasy from reality.
　　　　　　Example: Listen to *The Day Jimmy's Boa Ate the Wash,* Trinka Hakes Noble's story about a class field trip to a farm, and *Farming,* Gail Gibbons' nonfiction book about farming. Tell how these two books are different.

K.3.2　　Retell (beginning, middle, end) familiar stories.
　　　　　　Example: Retell the story of a folk tale, such as the version of *The Three Little Pigs* by Steven Kellogg.

K.3.3　　Identify characters, settings, or important events in a story (plot).
　　　　　　Example: Identify the main characters in a story, such as *Noisy Nora* by Rosemary Wells.
　　　　　　Describe the setting in a familiar story, such as *Goodnight Moon* by Margaret Wise Brown. Retell the important events in a story, such as the folk tale *Jack and the Beanstalk.*

K.3.4   Identify favorite books and stories.

K.3.4.A1   Understand what is heard or seen by responding to questions *(who, what, when, where, why, how)* and by using other appropriate comprehension strategies from Standard 2 such as responding to questions about context, predictions or conclusions, prior knowledge, or order (sequence).

Standard 4 — WRITING: Process

Students discuss ideas and tell stories for someone to write. Students use pictures, letters, and words to write.

Organization and Focus

K.4.1   Discuss ideas to include in a story.

K.4.2   Tell a story that the teacher or some other person will write.

K.4.3   Write using pictures, letters, and words.

K.4.4   Write phonetically spelled words (words that are written as they sound) and consonant-vowel-consonant words (demonstrating the alphabetic principle). Example: Write correctly simple words, such as *man, cat,* and *run,* and spell other words as they sound, such as *whale* as *wal, jumps* as *jmps,* and *bigger* as *bigr,* showing an understanding of what letters represent certain sounds.

K.4.5   Write by moving from left to right and from top to bottom.

Standard 5 — WRITING: Applications (Different Types of Writing and Their Characteristics)

In Kindergarten, students begin to write and draw pictures for specific purposes and for a specific audience (intended reader).

K.5.1   Draw pictures and write words for a specific reason.
Example: Draw a picture or write to a friend or a family member to tell about something new at school.

K.5.2   Draw pictures and write for specific people or persons.
Example: Write or dictate an invitation to a parent to attend a classroom event.

Standard 6 — WRITING: English Language Conventions

Students begin to learn the written conventions of Standard English.

Handwriting

K.6.1   Write capital and lowercase letters of the alphabet, correctly shaping and spacing the letters.

Spelling

K.6.2   Spell independently using an understanding of the sounds of the alphabet and knowledge of letter names.
Example: Spell correctly common words, such as *cat,* or spell by how the word sounds, such as *kat.*

LISTENING AND SPEAKING: Skills, Strategies, and Applications

Students listen and respond to oral communication. They speak in clear and coherent sentences. Students deliver brief oral presentations about familiar experiences or interests.

Comprehension

K.7.1   Understand and follow one- and two-step spoken directions.

Oral Communication

K.7.2   Share information and ideas, speaking in complete, coherent sentences.

Speaking Applications

K.7.3   Describe people, places, things (including their size, color, and shape), locations, and actions.

K.7.4   Recite short poems, rhymes, and songs.

K.7.5   Tell an experience or creative story in a logical sequence.

Looking Ahead: GRADE 2

Reading STREET

Grade **2**

Indiana

English/Language Arts

Academic Standards

READING: Word Recognition, Fluency, and Vocabulary Development

Students understand the basic features of words. They see letter patterns and know how to translate them into spoken language by using phonics (an understanding of the different letters that make different sounds), syllables, and word parts (-s, -ed, -ing). They apply this knowledge to achieve fluent (smooth and clear) oral and silent reading. They listen to stories read aloud to them or read books independently and use the vocabulary in their oral language and writing.

Phonemic Awareness

2.1.1   Demonstrate an awareness of the sounds that are made by different letters by:
• distinguishing beginning, middle, and ending sounds in words.
• rhyming words.
• clearly pronouncing blends and vowel sounds.

Decoding and Word Recognition

2.1.2   Recognize and use knowledge of spelling patterns (such as *cut/cutting, slide/sliding*) when reading.

2.1.3   Decode (sound out) regular words with more than one syllable (*dinosaur, vacation*).

2.1.4   Recognize common abbreviations (*Jan., Fri.*).

2.1.5   Identify and correctly use regular plural words (*mountain/mountains*) and irregular plural words (*child/children, mouse/mice*).

2.1.6   Read aloud fluently and accurately with appropriate changes in voice and expression.

2.1.6.A1   Know and use common word families (such as *-ale, -est, -ine, -ock, -ump*) when reading unfamiliar words.

Vocabulary and Concept Development

2.1.7   Understand and explain common synonyms (words with the same meaning) and antonyms (words with opposite meanings).

2.1.8   Use knowledge of individual words to predict the meaning of unknown compound words (*lunchtime, lunchroom, daydream, raindrop*).

2.1.8.A1   Read and understand more difficult root words (such as *chase*) and their inflectional forms (*chases, chased, chasing*).

2.1.9   Know the meaning of simple prefixes (word parts added at the beginning of words such as *un-*) and suffixes (word parts added at the end of words such as *-ful*).

2.1.10   Identify simple multiple-meaning words (*change, duck*).

2.1.10.A1 Listen to stories read aloud or read independently and use the vocabulary in oral language and writing.

Standard 2

READING: Comprehension and Analysis of Nonfiction and Informational Text

Students read and understand grade-level-appropriate material. They use a variety of comprehension strategies, such as asking and responding to essential questions, drawing conclusions or making predictions, and comparing information from several sources to understand what they read. The selections in the **Indiana Reading List** *(available online at www.doe.state.in.us/standards/readinglist.html) illustrate the quality and complexity of the materials to be read by students. In addition to their regular school reading, at Grade 2, students read a variety of grade-level-appropriate nonfiction and informational texts, such as books on science, social studies, mathematics and other subjects, children's magazines and periodicals, dictionaries and other reference or technical materials, and online information.*

Structural Features of Informational and Technical Materials

2.2.1   Use titles, tables of contents, and chapter headings to locate information in text.

2.2.1.A1   Identify text that uses sequence or other logical order (alphabetical order or time).

2.2.1.A2   Identify age-and-content-appropriate information online with the aid of a teacher or educator.

Analysis of Grade-Level-Appropriate Nonfiction and Informational Text

2.2.2   State the purpose for reading.
Example: Compare similar stories from different cultures, such as *Little Red Riding Hood* and *Lon Po Po* (Chinese version). Read an informational text about pets to decide what kind of animal would make the best pet.

2.2.3   Use knowledge of the author's purpose(s) to comprehend informational text.
Example: Read an informational text that compares different people, animals, or plants, such as *Gator or Croc* by Allan Fowler.

2.2.4   Ask and respond to questions *(why, what if, how)* to aid comprehension about important elements of informational texts.
Example: After reading a short account about the first man on the moon, ask and answer *why, what if,* and *how* questions to understand the lunar landing.

2.2.5   Restate facts and details or summarize the main idea in the text to clarify and organize ideas.
Example: Summarize information learned from a text, such as detail about ant colonies stated in *Ant Cities* by Arthur Dorros or reported about spider webs in *Spider Magic* by Dorothy Hinshaw Patent.

2.2.6   Recognize cause-and-effect relationships in a text.
Example: Read an informational book that explains some common scientific causes and effects, such as the growth of a plant from a seed or the effects of different weather patterns, such as too much snow or rain at one time causing flooding.

2.2.7   Interpret information from diagrams, charts, and graphs.
Example: Use a five-day weather chart or a weather chart on the Internet to determine the weather for the coming weekend.

2.2.8   Follow two-step written instructions.

2.2.8.A1   Understand or interpret what is read or heard by continuing to use comprehension strategies such as those involving context, drawing conclusions, or prior knowledge.

Reading-Nonfiction-on-Demand (Lifelong Learning Skill)

2.2.8.A2   Answer questions and write responses to a timed reading of short nonfiction or informational selections representing a wide range of grade-level-appropriate topics.

READING: Comprehension, Literary Response, and Analysis of Fiction

*Students read and respond to a wide variety of significant works of children's literature. They use comprehension strategies, such as identifying and discussing the characters, theme (the main message of a story), plot (what happens in a story), and the setting (where a story takes place) of stories that they read. The selections in the **Indiana Reading List** (available online at www.doe.state.in.us/standards/readinglist.html) illustrate the quality and complexity of the materials to be read by students. At Grade 2, students read a wide variety of fiction, such as classic and contemporary fiction, folk tales, poetry or songs, plays, and others.*

Literary Analysis of Grade-Level-Appropriate Text

2.3.1   Compare plots, settings, and characters presented by different authors.
Example: Read and compare *Strega Nona*, an old Italian folk tale retold by Tomie DePaola, with *Ox-Cart Man* by Donald Hall.

2.3.2   Create different endings to stories (predictions) and identify the reason (problem) and the impact of the different ending (solution).
Example: Read a story, such as *Fin M'Coul — The Giant of Knockmany Hill*, Tomie DePaola's retelling of an Irish folk tale. Then, discuss different possible endings to the story, such as how the story would change if Fin's wife had not helped him or if Fin were not a giant.

2.3.2.A1   Confirm predictions about what will happen next in a story.

2.3.3   Compare versions of same stories from different cultures.
Example: Compare fairy tales and folk tales that have been retold by different cultures, such as *The Three Little Pigs* and the southwestern/Latino version *The Three Little Javelinas* by Susan Lowell, or *Cinderella* and the African version, *Mufaro's Beautiful Daughters* by John Steptoe.

2.3.4   Identify the use of rhythm, rhyme, and alliteration (using words with repeating consonant sounds) in poetry or narratives (stories).
Example: Listen to or read the rhymes for each letter of the alphabet in *A, My Name Is Alice* by Jane Bayer. Tell what effects the writer uses to make the poems fun to hear.

2.3.4.A1   Recognize the difference between fantasy and reality.

2.3.4.A2   Discuss the author's main message (theme) of a story.

2.3.4.A3   Understand or interpret what is read or heard by responding to questions *(who, what, when, where, why, how)* and by using appropriate comprehension strategies from Standard 2, such as drawing conclusions, identifying the author's purpose, relating to prior knowledge, restating details, or setting a purpose for reading.

Reading-Fiction-on-Demand (Lifelong Learning Skill)

2.3.4.A4   Answer questions and write responses to a timed reading of short selections representing a wide range of literature on grade-level-appropriate topics or themes.

WRITING: Process

Students write clear sentences and paragraphs that develop a central idea. Students progress through the stages of the writing process, including prewriting, drafting, revising, and editing multiple drafts.

Organization and Focus

2.4.1   Create a list of ideas for writing.

2.4.2   Organize related ideas together to maintain a consistent focus.

Research and Technology

2.4.3   Find ideas for writing stories and descriptions in pictures or books.

2.4.4   Understand the purposes of various reference materials (such as a dictionary, thesaurus, or atlas).

2.4.5   Use a computer to draft, revise, and publish writing.

Standard
4

Evaluation and Revision

2.4.6   Review, evaluate, and revise writing for meaning and clarity.

2.4.7   Proofread one's own writing, as well as that of others, using an editing checklist or list of rules.

2.4.8   Revise original drafts to improve sequence (the order of events) or to provide more descriptive detail.

WRITING: Applications (Different Types of Writing and Their Characteristics)

At Grade 2, students are introduced to letter writing. Students continue to write compositions that describe and explain familiar objects, events, and experiences. Students continue to write simple rhymes and poems. Student writing demonstrates a command of Standard English and the drafting, research, and organizational strategies outlined in Standard 4—Writing Process. Writing demonstrates an awareness of the audience (intended reader) and purpose for writing.

Different Types of Writing and Their Characteristics

In addition to producing the different writing forms introduced in earlier grades, Grade 2 students use the writing strategies outlined in Standard 4—Writing Process to:

2.5.1   Write brief narratives (stories) based on their experiences that:
• move through a logical sequence of events.
• describe the setting, characters, objects, and events in detail.
Example: Write a story about an experience that took place during a certain season in the year: spring, summer, fall, or winter. Tell the story in the order that it happened and describe it in enough detail so that the reader can picture clearly the place, people, and events.

2.5.2   Write a brief description of a familiar object, person, place, or event that:
• develops a main idea.
• uses details to support the main idea.
Example: Write a descriptive piece on a topic, such as *Houses Come in Different Shapes and Sizes.*

2.5.3   Write a friendly letter complete with the date, salutation (greeting, such as *Dear Mr. Smith*), body, closing, and signature.
Example: Write a letter to the police department in your town asking if someone can come to your classroom to talk about bicycle safety.

2.5.4   Write rhymes and simple poems.

2.5.5   Use descriptive words when writing.

2.5.6   Write for different purposes and to a specific audience or person.
Example: Write a description of your favorite book to recommend the book to a friend.

2.5.6.A1   Write responses to literature that:
• demonstrate an understanding of what is read.
• support statements with references to both the text and prior knowledge.
Example: Write a description of a favorite character in a book. Include examples from the book to show why this character is such a favorite.

Writing-on-Demand (Lifelong Learning Skill)

2.5.6.A2   Write a first-draft, timed composition with a beginning, middle, and end for writing prompts that require narrative and descriptive writing.

WRITING: English Language Conventions

Students write using Standard English conventions appropriate to this grade level.

Handwriting

2.6.1   Form letters correctly and space words and sentences properly so that writing can be read easily by another person.

Sentence Structure

2.6.2   Distinguish between complete *(When Tom hit the ball, he was proud.)* and incomplete sentences *(When Tom hit the ball).*

2.6.3   Use the correct word order in written sentences.

Grammar

2.6.4   Identify and correctly write various parts of speech, including nouns (words that name people, places, or things) and verbs (words that express action or help make a statement).
Example: Identify the noun and verb in a sentence, such as *Maria* (noun) *and a friend* (noun) *played* (verb) *for a long time.*

Punctuation

2.6.5   Use commas in the greeting *(Dear Sam,)* and closure of a letter *(Love, or Your friend,)* and with dates *(March 22, 2000)* and items in a series *(Tony, Steve, and Bill).*

2.6.6   Use quotation marks correctly to show that someone is speaking.
• Correct: "You may go home now," she said.
• Incorrect: "You may go home now she said."

Capitalization

2.6.7   Capitalize all proper nouns (names of specific people or things, such as *Mike, Indiana, Jeep*), words at the beginning of sentences and greetings, months and days of the week, and titles *(Dr., Mr., Mrs., Miss)* and initials in names.

Spelling

2.6.8   Spell correctly words like *was, were, says, said, who, what,* and *why,* which are used frequently but do not fit common spelling patterns.

2.6.9   Spell correctly words with short and long vowel sounds *(a, e, i, o, u)*, r-controlled vowels *(ar, er, ir, or, ur)*, and consonant-blend patterns *(bl, dr, st).*
• short vowels: actor, effort, ink, chop, unless
• long vowels: ace, equal, bind, hoe, use
• *r*-controlled: park, supper, bird, corn, further
• consonant blends: blue, crash, desk, speak, coast

LISTENING AND SPEAKING: Skills, Strategies, and Applications

Students listen critically and respond appropriately to oral communication. They speak in a manner that guides the listener to understand important ideas by using proper phrasing, pitch, and modulation (raising and lowering voice). Students deliver brief oral presentations about familiar experiences or interests that are organized around a coherent thesis statement (a statement of topic). Students use the same Standard English conventions for oral speech that they use in their writing.

Comprehension

2.7.1 Determine the purpose or purposes of listening (such as to obtain information, to solve problems, or to enjoy).

2.7.2 Ask for clarification and explanation of stories and ideas.

2.7.3 Paraphrase (restate in own words) information that has been shared orally by others.

2.7.4 Give and follow three- and four-step oral directions.

Organization and Delivery of Oral Communication

2.7.5 Organize presentations to maintain a clear focus.

2.7.6 Speak clearly and at an appropriate pace for the type of communication (such as an informal discussion or a report to class).

2.7.7 Tell experiences in a logical order.

2.7.8 Retell stories, including characters, setting, and plot.

2.7.9 Report on a topic with supportive facts and details.

2.7.9.A1 Use descriptive words when speaking about people, places, things, and events.

Speaking Applications

2.7.10 Recount experiences or present stories that:
• move through a logical sequence of events.
• describe story elements, including characters, plot, and setting.

2.7.11 Report on a topic with facts and details, drawing from several sources of information.

2.7.11.A1 Recite poems, rhymes, songs, and stories.

2.7.11.A2 Provide descriptions with careful attention to sensory detail.

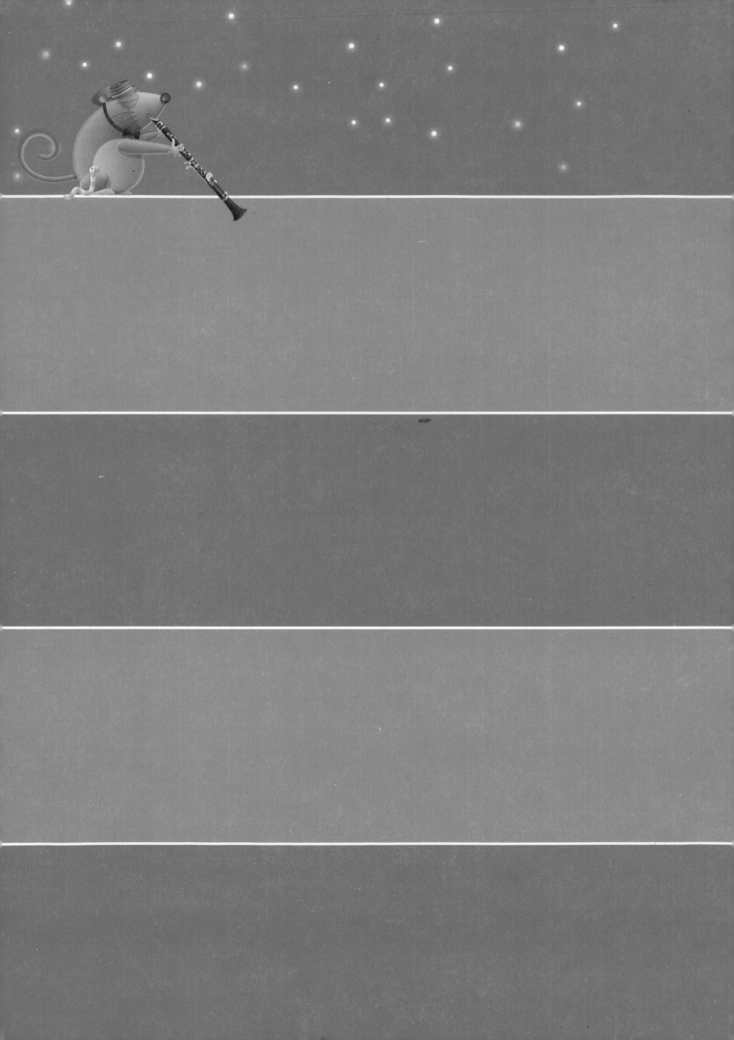